INSIDE THE MINDS

Intellectual Property Licensing Strategies

Leading Lawyers on Drafting IP Agreements, Negotiating Terms, and Evaluating Financial Implications

BOOK & ARTICLE IDEA SUBMISSIONS

If you are a C-Level executive, senior lawyer, or venture capitalist interested in submitting a book or article idea to the Aspatore editorial board for review, please email Hauthors@aspatore.comH. Aspatore is especially looking for highly specific ideas that would have a direct financial impact on behalf of a reader. Completed publications can range from 2 to 2,000 pages. Include your book/article idea, biography, and any additional pertinent information.

WRITING & EDITORIAL ASSISTANCE

In select instances Aspatore will assist in helping our authors generate the content for their publication via phone interviews. Aspatore editors create interview questions that help generate the main content for the book or article. The content from the phone interviews is then transcribed and edited for review and enhancement by the author. If this method could be of assistance in helping you find the time to write an article or book, please email Heditorial@aspatore.comH for more information, along with your biography and your publication idea.

Copyright © 2007 by Aspatore, Inc.
All rights reserved. Printed in the United States of America.

No part of this publication may be reproduced or distributed in any form or by any means, or stored in a database or retrieval system, except as permitted under Sections 107 or 108 of the U.S. Copyright Act, without prior written permission of the publisher. This book is printed on acid free paper.

Material in this book is for educational purposes only. This book is sold with the understanding that neither any of the authors or the publisher is engaged in rendering legal, accounting, investment, or any other professional service. Neither the publisher nor the authors assume any liability for any errors or omissions or for how this book or its contents are used or interpreted or for any consequences resulting directly or indirectly from the use of this book. For legal advice or any other, please consult your personal lawyer or the appropriate professional.

The views expressed by the individuals in this book (or the individuals on the cover) do not necessarily reflect the views shared by the companies they are employed by (or the companies mentioned in this book). The employment status and affiliations of authors with the companies referenced are subject to change.

Aspatore books may be purchased for educational, business, or sales promotional use. For information, please email store@aspatore.com or call 1-866-Aspatore.

ISBN 978-1-59622-793-4   Library of Congress Control Number: 2007931422

For corrections, updates, comments or any other inquiries please email editorial@aspatore.com.

First Printing, 2007
10 9 8 7 6 5 4 3 2 1

If you are interested in purchasing the book this chapter was originally included in, please call 1-866-Aspatore (277-2867) or visit www.Aspatore.com.

Licensing Technology and Content: Important Considerations

Richard E. Neff

*Partner and Chair, Intellectual Property
& Technology Department*
Greenberg Glusker Fields Claman & Machtinger LLP

My practice as an intellectual property lawyer is diverse and ever changing. Often, a client has an idea, or has created something that the client believes is original. This may be a Web site with exciting features or functionality, a concept for an online service, a computer software program, a lamp with a very interesting shape, a new kitchen implement, or a fashion item with some special design features. The client may believe that the idea or creation should be protected, and wants to discuss how to protect it. It may happen that the lamp or fashion design already has been copied by someone else, and the client wants to know what rights he or she has. The initial client meeting may cover such issues as whether the creation or invention or detailed concept should have a registered copyright or should be patented, what must be taken into consideration in order to protect it as a trade secret, and whether trademarks and service marks connected with it should be registered.

My bread and butter practice consists of representing software, technology and digital content companies (or users), and handling the drafting of agreements by which they license their technology or digital content to other parties. "Content" generally refers to text, graphics, and audio and video files that may be licensed to a Web site owner or operator for the latter's use. My clients license the technology and content because they do not want to give up ownership of it, so the right to use the product or technology or content and other rights acquired by the licensee are carefully circumscribed by contract. Nearly as often, I represent technology licensees who may be licensing systems from other technology companies, or they may be contracting with Web site developers to design a "killer" Web site.

Licensing is at the heart of any *intellectual property* or IP transactional practice. However, there are many transactions in which a company sells its technology or intellectual property, often when all or part of a company is sold to another company. If there is a substantial intellectual property component to the transaction, I may handle the entire transaction. More commonly, I work with my firm's corporate lawyers, and handle the intellectual property aspects of the transaction. For example, my firm recently sold a major video clip Web site to MTV. I had to negotiate with the buyer regarding the copyright situation of the seller's site, and also work on all of the IP representations and *warranties,* or promises, by the seller to the buyer, to ensure that these were promises that the seller could make and would not breach.

Another aspect of my practice is the protection and enforcement of intellectual property rights overseas, generally consisting of overseas copyright and/or trademark enforcement. From 1989 to 1995, I initiated many of the computer software industry's anti-piracy programs in Asia and most of the programs in Latin America, generally acting under the banner of the Business Software Alliance, the BSA. For about fifteen years I have run many of the Latin American anti-piracy programs for large computer software publishers (such as Microsoft, Adobe, Autodesk, and Symantec), generally acting in the name of the BSA. I also have run overseas anti-piracy/copyright enforcement programs for the Association of American Publishers, (AAP) in Latin America, and for the Interactive Digital Software Association (IDSA), predecessor to the Entertainment Software Association (ESA).

I tend to specialize in international aspects of intellectual property transactions, and in addition to handling overseas enforcement, many of my licensing and other deals involve international issues, often a license agreement between a U.S. licensor and an overseas licensee. In recent years this has included various outsourcing agreements for technology development or even call centers. In addition, I frequently advise and opine about foreign laws, especially foreign copyright laws or privacy laws of other countries.

Finally, I advise clients on copyright issues. For example, a Web site client serving as an online or Internet service provider might want to know whether it is obligated to check every video that users upload to the site for infringement or other issues (e.g., defamation, inappropriate, or pornographic content). The Digital Millennium Copyright Act, amendments to U.S. Copyright Law, is instructive on this point. Another client created a Bill of Rights sculpture for the McCormick Tribune Freedom Museum in Chicago, with a thousand "freedom" quotations, and we had to advise on the client's right to use each of the quotations.

All my clients have intellectual property needs. Often these are needs they have identified, but there may be many needs of which they are unaware, and the client's wish list may be limited by budgetary concerns. In addition, it is very useful to minimize risk, but ultimately clients are in business to make money, which entails some degree of risk. What I try to do is calibrate a response based on the value of the client's intellectual property, the client's exposure, and the client's budget.

Many intellectual property lawyers fail to bring a business perspective to their client counseling. I always try to give advice that takes into account both clients' business and legal needs. For example, every client has a brand, whether a product or a name, that is worth protecting. However, there is no point counseling them to consider a community trademark (CTM) in Europe if they have no plans to have a strong presence in Europe. Their early stage expenditures can best be made elsewhere. If you understand your client's business, you'll know what risks are worth protecting against, and which are a cost of doing business. However, given a career-long focus on technology and Internet transactions, it generally is clear to me which issues are important and which are not worth fighting for.

When advising clients, many issues arise related to intellectual property rights. What follows are some of the most important ones.

Identification of IP Assets and the Right Form of Protection

Depending upon the nature of the client, an initial meeting may raise issues about what assets the client has to protect, and the proper form of protection, especially with smaller clients or early stage companies. Large corporate clients generally know what they have and what they want to protect, within broad parameters. For example, clients not focused on intellectual property, such as a real estate developer or broker, might not give adequate attention to the value of its trade name and logo, and the need to act expeditiously to protect them. Real-life examples of the need to identify the issues and then prescribe the right protection include: (i) a client who thought her beautifully made and somewhat unique line of tote bags was being infringed by another line of tote bags, which had some similar features, and (ii) a client whose line of sculptural brass lamps appeared to have been knocked off by one of the country's largest retailers. What can be done in these cases? Both examples implicate such issues as whether copyright protection is available in either case, and if so, what needs to be done, whether trademark or trade dress protection is available, whether a design patent can be obtained. However, even a very large profitable and nationally known Internet company did not realize that its Web site could be registered with the Copyright Office, which proved very useful when other companies tried to copy the site virtually lock, stock, and barrel.

Ownership of Intellectual Property

In many technology and licensing deals, the ownership of intellectual property is a hot-button issue. A typical scenario involves a third party Web site developer who has been hired to build a "killer" e-commerce Web site for an Internet company (or even for a more traditional brick-and-mortar business). This would appear to be a simple "work-for-hire" agreement; the e-commerce company is paying the Web site developer for its time, and expects to own the result, the work product. But, in fact, the Web developer may use the same technology tools and modules over and over, not to mention the learning contained in the developer's head. You hire someone for their experience, not to reinvent the wheel. So maybe the e-commerce company cannot have absolute ownership of every bit of deliverables/work product. In a different scenario, if the Web developer will also be the Web host, which happens often, and if the e-commerce company is not well represented by counsel, the developer/Web host may claim a copyright in its creation, which might mean that it is difficult for the e-commerce company to change Web hosts, often a serious problem. Similarly, when two software companies are working together to ensure that their products are compatible, and APIs (applications programming interfaces) are developed to link the two programs, who owns the APIs? In many technology deals, getting ownership right is among the most difficult issues, not generally with core products where ownership may be clear, but at the margins.

Open Source Software

Closely related to the ownership issue is the issue of open source software, which surprises large and small technology companies alike, and affects any company that acquires systems and software. On the most basic level, let's assume Company A, which is a supermarket chain, not at all an IP-based company in the popular mind, is being sold to Company B. Company A will be asked to represent and warrant in the purchase agreement that it needs no consents or permissions (other than the list of consents which has been attached to the agreement) in order to guarantee that it is not infringing the intellectual property rights of any person, that it is not in breach of any agreements, and perhaps that all of its software is properly licensed. However, developers have done a lot of customization on Company A's (the supermarket chain) enterprise-wide software system that runs its inventory, accounting, and sales registers. It turns out that the developers have incorporated a lot of open source software components into Company A's network, without paying any attention to such licenses as the Apache and GNU general public license that may govern the use of such modules. This happens all the time, and this may put the seller in breach of its representations and warranties in the purchase and sale agreement with Company B. Even software companies have a hard time complying with all of the licenses for the open source code used in their development efforts. This area requires careful lawyering, as inattention to legal detail can result in triggering the viral aspects of open source licenses, and turning all of a company's proprietary code into open source software. To explain more fully, when certain open source software subject to such licenses as the GNU General Public License is combined with proprietary software, the aggregated software may all be subject to the GNU General Public License, and therefore, all effectively may have become open source software.

Limiting Liability and Indemnity

While clients are often focused on ownership, their eyes tend to glaze over when focusing on this most legalistic of issues (along with warranty disclaimers): limiting liability and the indemnity provisions. Generally, the party with the most leverage in a deal tries to limit its own liability as much as possible, while leaving the opposing party's liability and indemnification obligations unlimited to the maximum extent possible. So, the battle on these issues is often over leverage, as opposed to over right and wrong. An example of a licensor-friendly limitation of liability provision can be found in the software license and service agreement attached hereto as Appendix A. In Section 11(e) of that agreement, the licensor's sole obligation in the event of a defect in the licensed software is to repair or replace such software, and only if the licensor is unable to achieve repair or replacement must the licensee be reimbursed for its license fees, in this case for any fees paid during the prior twelve months for the defective portion of the licensed software. I would expect some push-back from the licensee over this provision, although its essence (repair, replacement or refund) is industry standard in this context.

In addition, the technology licensor in a deal generally is expected to hold the licensee harmless from any claims that the technology being licensed infringes a third party's intellectual property rights, on the basic theory that the licensor, which owns and/or created the technology, is in a much better position than the licensee to know, or to have figured out, whether its technology infringes third party rights. A sample provision can be found in the license agreement attached hereto as Appendix A, in which each party must indemnify the other party against any third party claims concerning the infringement by the indemnifying party's software of the rights of any third party. To the extent the licensed software is owned by the indemnifying party, the indemnifying party has an obligation to indemnify. However, in the sample provision, written from the licensor perspective, the obligation is limited to infringement of third party rights arising in the United States. This may be too narrow an indemnity obligation from the licensee perspective. In some instances, the licensor may try to impose a "to the best of knowledge" standard on the indemnity obligation, on the theory that it is still hard to know what unknown development or invention will suddenly appear in the future whose owner claims that the licensor's technology infringes its earlier-created technology.

The difficulty in the United States is that the U.S. Patent and Trademark Office, unlike most of its counterparts around the world, has spent more than a decade issuing software patents and business methods patents, probably much too broadly and without adequate care. These patents are often used by their owners in an aggressive, sometimes extortionate manner against unsuspecting technology, Internet and other companies. In fact, many smaller companies buy up patent portfolios simply to use them as swords against legitimate companies, such companies are now referred to as "patent trolls." The patent risk to all parties has become extreme, because of the exorbitant defense costs, making negotiations over the extent of the indemnity a difficult (and sometimes hostile) issue. Parties to an agreement will often haggle over how broad-based the indemnity should be, e.g., should the indemnity be limited to third-party claims arising in the United States? Should a licensee indemnify and hold the licensor harmless from claims arising from its use of the technology beyond the scope of the license? What about damage to persons and property? All of these issues must be addressed.

Source Code Escrow

In technology licenses, when one company licenses software from another company, the issue of whether the licensor's source code should be placed in escrow for the benefit of the licensee often surfaces. Source code is the human readable version of the machine readable object code, which is compiled into object code containing a sequence of instructions which a processor can understand. Basically, the licensee takes the position that, should certain triggering events occur, it will need access to the licensor's source code to support the software it is using (and possibly, depending on the license rights granted, to modify it). Only the object code version of software is usually licensed in other than development licenses. The licensor should have an existing contract with an escrow company, and the licensee typically enters into an addendum to that contract, becoming a beneficiary of that escrow agreement.

When I represent the licensor, I may initially resist a source code escrow, although escrowing software is an accepted practice. If required, I may try to have the licensee pay for the incremental escrow costs, since the escrow is for the benefit of the licensee.

Once it is agreed that there will be a source code escrow for the benefit of the licensee, the key issue generally surrounds what constitutes a trigger event which will cause the escrow agent to release the source code to the licensee. Generally, bankruptcy and related insolvency constitute the baseline escrow release event, which may present both legal and practical problems. Legally, the removal of the licensor's source code from escrow upon a bankruptcy filing by the licensor may be unenforceable, if it were held to violate the automatic stay as an act against the property of the licensor-debtor. In practical terms, if a reorganizing debtor-licensor is able to render adequate support, there may be no good reason for an escrow release, and the licensee may not be in any position to either render support or modify the source code, never having worked with the source code.

When I represent a licensee client, I insist that failure of the licensor to adequately support the licensed software should be a release trigger. This generally kicks off a negotiation over what constitutes inadequate support. In practical terms, access of the licensee to escrowed source code may be less useful than it appears, as there is no guarantee that the source code will be readily useable by the licensee, that the source code is up to date and clearly commented, or that licensee's personnel will have the necessary experience to utilize the source code effectively. In any event, ordinarily the licensee's rights in the source code should never exceed the rights that it had in the object code.

Privacy and Data Transfer

The bundle of issues surrounding personal privacy and data transfer did not really exist fifteen years ago. But since then, there have been two major developments in the world. First, the rise of the Internet has made personal information and data ubiquitous, much too available in the opinion of many. Second, European countries and the European Union passed very strong protections for personally identifiable information, which have been copied by other countries, such as Canada.[1] Even U.S. clients need to be very careful in this area, or they may face sanctions. An example of a transaction that could ensnare a U.S. company in European legal proceedings would be if a U.S. company were to buy another U.S. company that has a French subsidiary, after which the buyer transfers all the information about the acquired company employees, including those in the French subsidiary (which information resides on French servers), to its servers in San Diego. If the French workforce has not expressly consented to this transfer, French privacy law most likely has been violated. The worldwide trend is toward stronger protection of personal information, and this has many pitfalls for clients.

---

[1] Strong privacy protections do exist in certain sectors of the US economy, such as health care and financial information.

There are various components of intellectual property law that are important to nearly all of my clients. Here I will describe some of the major ones.

Identification of Intellectual Property Issues and Protection

For less experienced clients, start-ups, and smaller companies, identification of the appropriate intellectual property protection is the place to begin. For example, in the case of the client that produces unique lamps, in addition to advising on issues of trademark protection in the U.S. and around the world, we advised them on the availability of copyright and design protection to prevent knockoffs.

Drafting Documents for the Appropriate Business Model

Some clients need to have documents or terms of use drafted because their business model is evolving or changing. For example, a software company that traditionally shipped "boxes" (packaged software) decided to offer a hosted software-as-a-service or ASP model, and asked me to draft the license agreement or terms of use that would govern the new service business model. In another case, a major Hollywood studio was moving toward providing films and film clips to subscribers on an on-demand basis using BitTorrent technology, the peer-to-peer digital content delivery platform, and asked me to draft the license terms.

Doing the Deal: Licensing or Purchase/Sale

We get involved when a client has a particular deal in mind, such as licensing its technology to a larger company in a better position to market it, or selling assets it no longer needs (e.g., one client no longer needed its insurance leads Web site, and I drafted the asset sale agreement, covering the Web site, some content, some related software, and an extensive customer list). Another client was a well-known video upload site which was being purchased by one of the major national media companies, and I handled the intellectual property due diligence in the deal, which involved a lot of negotiation over copyright representations and warranties.

Intellectual Property Theft in the U.S. and Around the World

Some clients approach us when they believe their intellectual property is being stolen or copied or counterfeited abroad, as we have special expertise in handling such issues. Our correspondent IP counsel around the world have worked with us on many significant anti-piracy programs for the computer software, books, and computer or digital games industries.

Latin America Specialty

Finally, while I handle deals and enforcement all over the world, I have a specialty in doing legal work and intellectual property protection in Latin America, where I lived and in effect practiced for many years. I speak Spanish and Portuguese. For example, I have run most of the larger software companies' anti-piracy programs through the auspices of the Business Software Alliance, acting for Microsoft, Adobe, Autodesk, Symantec and Apple, among others. I also handle the negotiation of many of the digital download deals for a prominent mobile games publishing client, with the leading wireless carriers in Latin America. These deals are done entirely in Spanish or Portuguese. For other technology companies, I have negotiated numerous deals with large Latin American banks, oil, and mining companies, including with large Latin American state-owned enterprises, particularly in Mexico and Brazil. I also handle copyright and policy issues for clients in Latin America, e.g., one large software publisher wanted to know if it could default to automatic renewal of its subscription service for clients located in Latin America, and asked us to do a twenty-five country survey. In fact, Microsoft and/or the BSA engaged me to comment on most copyright law reforms in Latin America over a period of more than ten years, and my language can be found in several such laws, so I tend to be familiar with Latin American and other countries' copyright (authors' rights) laws.

Financial Implications of Intellectual Property

The value of intellectual property to the U.S. economy is extraordinary, and growing. For example, the International Intellectual Property Alliance (IIPA) estimated that in 2005, the *core* copyright industries (software, film, books, music, and distribution of same) accounted for $819.06 billion in revenues, or 6.56 percent of the overall United States gross domestic product(GDP).[2] If the definition of copyright industries is expanded, the total copyright industries generated $1.38 trillion in revenues that year, or 11.12 percent of GDP.[3] If one adds the tremendous contribution of patent-based industries to the U.S. economy, such as pharmaceutical, chemical, and manufacturing sectors, the extraordinary value of intellectual property is readily apparent.

Enhancing Intellectual Property Value for Clients

The value of intellectual property, which is intangible property, may not be readily apparent to new clients. For example, we recently sold a major video clip upload site to one of the major media companies. The owners of the Web site probably did not anticipate that one day it would sell for many millions of dollars, one of many illustrations of the value of intangible property in the Internet age. Much of the due diligence turned on the copyright status of the content, which consisted of tens of thousands of video clips. To some extent, the more rights that the sellers of the site had obtained prior to sale of the Web site to the copyrighted material on the Web site, the more value the site would have to the buyers.

Another example of enhancing the value of intellectual property was convincing the owners of a very successful e-commerce site, which ultimately sold for hundreds of millions of dollars, to register the copyright in the Web site at an early stage. The copyright proved essential in sending cease and desist letters to copycat sites, and forcing them to close down. By taking such efforts to preserve the value of the growing brand, the Web site was able to increase in value and sell for a fortune.

Much of what I do involves technology or content license agreements. A good agreement from the technology or content licensor's perspective would aim to ensure that a client's liability for patent or copyright

---

[2] S. Siwek, Copyright Industries in the U.S. Economy: Economists Incorporated, prepared for the IIPA.
[3] "Core" copyright industries are those copyright-related industries whose primary purpose is to produce and or distribute copyright materials. The "total" copyright industries include 4 categories, "core," partial, non-dedicated support and interdependent sectors.

infringement is limited. Such limitation may save the client millions of dollars, should a patent claim arise. On the other hand, a good agreement from the technology or content licensee's perspective would aim to ensure that the licensee has limited exposure for using technology or content provided by the licensor. So the effective assistance of counsel very much affects the allocation of financial risk with respect to intellectual property claims.

In the trademark area, it makes tremendous sense to search carefully when choosing corporate names, domain names, and product names, so that the brand strategy can be coordinated from the start. The often penny-wise but pound-foolish practice of start-up ventures is just to use names that appeal to them, and find out later, in the face of cease and desist letters and threatened litigation, that a URL or domain name cannot be used because of a third party's superior trademark rights in a name or word that forms part of the URL, and that product names have to be changed, which is all very costly.

Getting one's trademark and domain name at the outset is important to avoid having to change product names or seek new domain names. There is no doubt that the trademark and domain name realms are increasingly crowded, with seemingly few desirable names or words still available for registration. For many companies, an overall intellectual property strategy should be adopted at a very early stage.

Pitfalls in Establishing Intellectual Property Value

A recent client problem serves a good illustration of the importance of making the right moves at the outset. An inventor devised a very attractive and useful add-on device for an MP3 player (the *product*). He allowed certain individuals, his *initial sellers*, without any contract whatsoever, to make and sell several thousand products, and then the inventor gave "exclusive" rights to other individuals, who have invested a lot of money in his product, to be his *exclusive sellers*. The exclusive sellers applied for a design patent, and also registered illustrations depicting the products with the U.S. Copyright Office.

Someone, possibly related to the initial sellers, or the initial sellers themselves, have been flooding the market with very inexpensive copies of his product. The exclusive sellers sought our assistance with bringing an infringement action against the initial sellers, or whoever was selling the knockoffs at that time. However, the patent had not issued, and will not issue for at least a year. Registering the illustrations could prevent one from copying them, but anyone who builds the product, without reference to the illustrations, probably is not liable for copyright infringement. The inventor had no written contract with the initial sellers. The absence of a contract that would protect the intellectual property in the product from reverse engineering or disclosure means that trade secret protection is most likely unavailable. The exclusive sellers do not have much recourse until the patent is issued, and by then, they already may have lost their market for the product. Had the inventor not given some shady individuals the right to make and distribute a certain number of copies without a contract, and had the exclusive sellers done some more due diligence and ensured that the product could still benefit from trade secret protection until the patent was published, the exclusive sellers might have been in a better position to ensure their future success.

Both smaller and more sophisticated technology companies often fail to segregate their use of open source software code from their use of proprietary software code. This creates a strong risk that even well-known software products are not in licensing compliance with all of their open source licenses. In the worst case, their proprietary software may become *infected* by the viral nature of certain open source software licenses. This means that the client's proprietary software may become impossible to segregate from the open source software, all of which may be governed by the open source license, and thus the company may have unwillingly surrendered ownership of its core asset, proprietary software.

In the case of upload sites for video and audio files, even well-known sites (such as YouTube) may neglect to give proper attention to the copyright status of the files displayed on the Web site. This can mean that the site potentially is infringing the rights of thousands of copyright holders. While registering under the DMCA with the Copyright Office and implementing a very responsive notice-and-takedown policy might insulate the site from copyright liability, it is increasingly likely that a more proactive procedure for screening third-party uploads will be required if such sites are to avoid being found to be direct infringers or contributory infringers under an evolving Grokster doctrine. Finally, all companies that license technology from others need to pay careful attention to contract terms and give thought to such important issues as: Who should own any development done for a licensee? And, if the licensee owns it, what right will the developer have to do similar development for other licensees? How easily should the parties be able to get out of the contract? Who should bear infringement liability, and should it be unlimited? And last, what acts or omissions should be indemnified by each party?

Right now I am counseling a large, sophisticated software company that licensed its technology from a licensor some years ago, and agreed to a long-term contract with no "outs" except for material breach. Each year my client pays large nonrefundable minimum royalties to the licensor. The licensor now has licensed technology that directly competes with my client's technology. This means that my client has more difficulty selling the combined product, as it directly competes with the licensor's combined product. The language of the contract does not permit my client to stop paying the minimum royalties. The right to escape payment of the minimum royalties or even to terminate the contract in the event that my client might face direct competition from its licensor should have been anticipated by the drafter of the original contract.

Personal Strategies for the Licensing Lawyer

The intake role is most important with start-up clients and clients who are less sophisticated. My role is comparable to that of a doctor doing medical intake on a new patient: a doctor would listen to the patient state what the patient's concerns may be, and what the problem is. Like the doctor, I then apply my expert prism to the company or individual at hand, determining the forms of protection that are necessary but may not have been considered by the client, and other issues the client may not have foreseen. Many Internet clients running Web sites where customers post items, such as audio files, video files, other content and e-commerce items, rarely know how to insulate themselves from infringement liability under the Digital Millennium Copyright Act. In such cases, I always suggest that they let me counsel them on how to position themselves, including how much vetting of third-party content they should do, and I ask them to let me register them with the Copyright Office for purposes of notice and takedown. I try to ensure that clients register their intellectual property, from trademarks to copyrights to filing applications for different types of patents, as early as possible. This generally protects the clients and helps to monetize their intellectual property. I also encourage them not to share any "great ideas" or technology or innovations except under tightly drafted nondisclosure agreements, both to protect their ideas, and also to preserve their trade secrets. I have developed clear licensing guidelines, which I apply in the appropriate context.

Keeping up on new developments is very challenging in the intellectual property and technology areas, as technology evolves very rapidly. I try to keep up on new developments through subscriptions to various online services and reading various digests and reports such as *Electronic Commerce & Law Report, Computer & Internet Lawyer, The Hollywood Reporter Esq.*, and *IP Law 360*. A major incentive to keep up is that my clients speak in an ever-changing techno-geek language that consists of various letters and numbers. One client is a leader in ETL technology, and is moving into BI software.[4] A number of clients are in the CRM space. SaaS is a very hot topic in the ASP world. Programming languages are 3GL, 4GL, even 5GL. Open source software may be subject to the GNU GPL. We were excited when cellular communications were 3G, and that is being made obsolete by 4G networks, etc. Now we're into Web 2.0, conceived of as the second generation of web-based communities and hosted services. My goal is to just keep up with new developments, in order to be able to follow client discussions, and also to be able to respond to reporters who call for commentary.

Licensing Strategies

The line of questioning for new clients at the first meeting varies with the nature of the client. For the start-up company that may have an

---

[4] Extract, Transform, Load. The other abbreviations or acronyms in this paragraph are: Business Intelligence, Customer Relationship Management, Software as a Service, Applications Service Provider, GNU General Public License, Third Generation Language, Fourth Generation Language, Fifth Generation Language, Third Generation, Fourth Generation.

unsophisticated understanding of intellectual property rights, my *modus operandi* is to inquire about the nature of their business, what their business model is (this may change over time), where they are in their development cycle, where they think they are headed, and what competitive forces they face. In short, much of the information I am gathering is the sort that an investor would want. It is information that should be, or will be, in any offering document or prospectus that the company prepares. The reason for taking the inquiry to this level is that only by having a reasonably deep understanding of the business, and the resources available to the company, can one fashion an appropriate intellectual property strategy. For example, if the company has no plans over the next five years to export to the European Union, then trying to convince the client at this point to register a relatively costly *community trademark* may be misguided.

With larger clients, or clients that are more evolved and developed, I may not obtain such detailed general information, as my engagement may be very specific in nature. Often they come to me simply to draft an agreement or to negotiate a deal. Some of my recent deals have included soundstage development technology for a major worldwide television network; development of motion-capture technology for a film studio; numerous online banking authentication software licenses for major financial institutions; deals facilitating mobile game download for users of mobile phones on various Latin American wireless networks; and drafting software-as-a-service agreements for a box software publisher moving into hosted subscription services.

For several of the clients described above, I have negotiated numerous deals, and over time, I learned the client's particular deal or licensing *religion*. The guidelines differ from client to client, and some of them turn to me to advise them on what guidelines to establish. One of these clients never agrees to take on unlimited infringement liability, and will reject a deal rather than have unlimited exposure of any kind. This client also requires non-solicitation clauses with its customers (so that their well-trained technicians cannot easily be poached). Another of these clients, negotiating with wireless carriers accustomed to offering non-negotiable terms on a take-it-or-leave-it basis, obviously has to incur some risk or no deals would ever close. In every case, the more I know about the client, the better I can protect its interests. In the initial transactions, I must interview the client in detail and consult frequently. On later deals, sometimes I speak with the client only on major issues or potential deal breakers that arise. However, even if the client fails to advise me adequately, or does not know how to advise me, I impose my own guidelines, which may vary based on the relative leverage that the client has in the deal. My guidelines should enable the client to close the deal but only on terms that are within the client's particular risk profile.

If a start-up client has designed a business plan, this can be very useful in helping me to understand the client's business model and goals. Sometimes I help draft a business plan, and cover the intellectual property issues in such plan. A more evolved client may have an offering document or prospectus, and this is very useful to the lawyer to assist in understanding the client. Any applications for intellectual property registration that the client has prepared will be useful for many client inquiries. Copies of patents or patent applications, a list of trademark filings and registrations, and a list of copyright registrations will all be useful.

For Internet and Web site clients, it is easy enough to access and print copies of the relevant Web site terms of use and privacy policy, if they exist. Very often clients want these policies created, or modified, or we advise the client that the policies need to be modified, based on legal requirements or changed facts or circumstances that I need to explore in detail with the client. For some clients I conduct a contract audit. I review all of their agreements, from relatively simple confidentiality and non-disclosure agreements, to development agreements, various distribution agreements and end user license agreements, including both print copies and *click-wrap* online versions, as well as other distribution, license, and support agreements. Generally clients provide me with copies of all agreements they seek to have modified or re-drafted. Often I am asked to internationalize U.S. agreements, as this is one of my specialties. Again, while I only need to see the U.S. agreements, I must interview the client extensively about where and how they will do business abroad.

Battle of the Forms

Finally, when negotiating license deals, the client will usually provide me with either its own license agreement, unless I have drafted it, or with the opposing party's form. Generally, it is far better for the client to do a deal on its own paper. Beginning with the adversary's documentation always creates an uphill battle to reach acceptable deal terms. This is often not apparent to clients, who are understandably focused on the high cost of premium legal services, and they sometimes view documentation from the other side of a transaction as a potentially huge cost saving. Clients are disappointed at the amount of negotiation required to modify the opposing party's documentation to make it acceptable. The software license and service agreement attached hereto as Appendix A is written from the licensor perspective, and most likely the licensee will want some changes, but in many respects it is a balanced agreement.

Why License Rather than Sell?

Technology, often a euphemism for software although it can encompass hardware too, tends to be licensed rather than sold. It is worth exploring why. The simple reason for this odd legal structure is that the owner of the software does not wish to part with ownership. The user, or licensee, only gets some attributes of ownership, but not others. While other copyrightable subject matter, such as art, books, music, and movies, may be sold to the user, software is licensed to the user. One key reason is to avoid the so-called *first sale doctrine*. Once a work is sold in commerce, known as the first sale, the seller cannot control subsequent dispositions of the article. With software, often the user or licensee cannot, because of restrictive license terms, sell or subsequently dispose of the software. The licensor still controls that right. For a good discussion of why technology is licensed rather than sold, please see the discussion of that issue in Appendix C attached hereto, "Key Technology Licensing Terms."

More generally, the owner of the software, which might be the result of millions of dollars of research and development, or in the case of some of the largest software publishers, such as Microsoft, billions of dollars worth of R&D, does not want to let the user own the software or make certain uses of it. The license generally cuts back the rights that the user would have by copyright, although the license may also extend certain rights. For example, the license may give a reseller the right to make 100,000 copies of a master copy of the software, something copyright law certainly does not permit. ·

Licenses run from a single page to dozens of pages in length. In most cases, they have the operative and unique license grant provisions up front (unless definitions come first), followed by payment provisions, after which come the warranty, limitation of liability, indemnity and termination provisions, followed by certain more "boilerplate" provisions such as governing law and notice provisions. Support and maintenance may be in a separate exhibit, a separate agreement, or covered in the main license itself.

I represent both licensors and licensees, and the strategic and tactical arguments vary, depending upon which side is the client. But the amount of leverage a party has is terribly important in determining whether a fair deal results. Some countries, such as those of the European Union, abhor unequal bargaining power, unconscionable provisions, and contracts of adhesion, where a party, as in a click-wrap or shrink-wrap scenario, is basically in a take-it-or-leave-it scenario.[5] But in the more Darwinian United States, private parties have the "liberty" to make virtually whatever bargain they want, which may be the bargain that the more powerful party wants. The largest software companies such as Oracle and Microsoft are renowned for not giving much room for their licensees to maneuver. On the other hand, powerful technology licensees, such as large banks and wireless carriers, often dictate the terms they will accept in technology licenses.

Issues to Consider in Licensing

The following are some considerations in negotiating license terms.

License Grant

The scope of the license grant obviously is important, and may be said to be the heart of the license. This is a provision that must be carefully discussed with the client, to determine whether the licensee gets development rights, manufacturing rights, distribution rights, or just the right to use the software internally. This provision tends to encompass both business and legal considerations.

---

[5] For an example of a click-wrap terms of use license, please see Appendix B attached hereto.

If the license involves software, is the licensee given source code, which is typical in a license in which the licensee is granted the right to modify the software and create derivative works, or is the licensee given only object code, which generally means that the software cannot be modified by the licensee. Almost all "user" licenses are object code licenses; for example, Microsoft certainly does not intend that you'll be modifying the underlying code in your Microsoft Word program.

Generally, the license grant provision, or a subsequent provision possibly called "Restrictions" or "Limitations", sets forth various restrictions in the license grant. For example, the license grant or a restrictions provision may state that you may only make a single copy of the licensed software for backup or archival purposes, although you may be able to copy the software onto a substitute system for backup or emergency testing or use, provided the software is only in operational use on the system for which it was licensed. Section 3 of the software license agreement attached hereto as Appendix A contains a fairly typical license grant provision for licensed software that is not intended to be developed or modified by the licensee, although there is the implication that the licensee has some rights to "adapt" the licensed software. The licensee is given permission to make a sufficient number of backup copies for archival purposes, but only so many as the licensee actually needs. This is a reasonable provision. Section 3(d) of Appendix A sets forth a well-written list of the restrictions on licensee's use of the licensed software.

Similarly, there will be language prohibiting the licensee from "disassembling, decompiling or reverse engineering" technology or software. However, this restriction has been perceived as problematic when a licensee of technology has been unable to use licensor's program with its other system software, in other words, to make licensor's software interoperable with other licensee software. Consequently, the European Union enacted the Software Directive in 1991, which permitted decompilation (deriving source code from object code) to achieve interoperability of programs, subject to various restrictions on such decompilation (e.g., if the licensor makes available information on achieving interoperability). A tightly drafted provision can avoid any problems that the licensor may face, such as only permitting decompilation when information on interoperability is unavailable from the licensor, and requiring that the licensee permit the licensor to be present during any such activity.

Acceptance and Payment

The payment provisions tend to fall more on the business side of the ledger, but a good lawyer can be very helpful in setting royalty rates, and if the lawyer represents the licensee, he or she can try to avoid mandatory minimum royalties. Moreover, if the contract involves code or technology development by one party for the other party, then the contract probably will have acceptance provisions that trigger payment obligations. The acceptance provisions will be more or less stringent depending in part on which party has leverage in the transaction. The lawyer advising the client must be familiar with the accounting provisions on software revenue recognition, as tough acceptance provisions may delay acceptance for periods of time that are unacceptable to the developer or licensor. Generally, there are only a handful of legal, as opposed to business, provisions in the payments area where the parties may be at loggerheads.

Ownership

The ownership issue may not be at all contentious in a straight technology license, where the licensee receives content or technology from the licensor for its use. However, as soon as the licensee has rights to modify or create derivative works of the technology it is licensing, or even to create calls or APIs (applications programming interfaces) to link a licensor program to a licensee or third party program, ownership issues come to the fore. In all development scenarios, ownership is an important issue. In the software license agreement attached as Appendix A, the licensee plans to use but not further develop the licensed software, so the ownership section, Section 9, is not controversial; the licensed software remains the property of the licensor. Difficult ownership issues are much more common in development and co-development transactions.

Term and Termination

The term of the agreement is very important, as is the ease with which the agreement can be terminated, and whether or not there will be renewal terms. It may be very difficult for a licensee if a licensor has the right to terminate an agreement for convenience. Automatic renewal with a long advance notice period, such as the requirement that either party must indicate that it does not wish to renew at least 180 days prior to a one-year renewal term, may force the unwitting party into a renewal term it does not want, because it has failed to object prior to 180 days before renewal.

Given an increasing tendency to license technology as a service on a subscription service model (often renewed on an annual basis, and requiring annual, quarterly or monthly payments), licensees are more often faced with a future inability to use software, as opposed to the traditional license model, in which the user generally has the right (absent breach) to use software under license in perpetuity. However, even with perpetual license terms, given the need that the software be supported, often both parties shared the view that use probably would not be perpetual. After all, support agreements generally are on an annual basis, and with rapid change in the technology world, it is rare that a user realistically expects to use an unsupported software program for more than a decade.

In the software license and service agreement attached hereto as Appendix A, the term is stated in Section 2 as five years. This agreement is a subscription service model, in which access to the software and support is paid for annually (but on a monthly basis) as a subscription. While the termination provisions in Section 12 are fairly standard, they have to be viewed in the context of annual subscription fees to be paid by the licensee for continued use of the software.

Warranty

Technology license warranties tend to have fairly standard language that the licensor warrants that the licensed software will perform substantially in accordance with documentation or specifications, and that implied warranties of merchantability and fitness for a particular purpose are expressly disclaimed. Sometimes implied warranties of non-infringement and title are also disclaimed. It tends to be unreasonable for the licensee to accept an "as is" warranty from the licensor in most circumstances; such a warranty essentially means that the licensor warrants nothing, similar to a "quitclaim deed" in a real estate context. For a fuller explanation of the meanings of these implied warranties, please see Appendix C attached hereto, called "Key Technology Licensing Terms" which contains a discussion of warranties.

The warranty is probably less important than it seems at first glance. First, technology contracts often have maintenance and support components, so the issue of warranty support may be subsumed into contractual support. However, sometimes warranty support is free support, or an opportunity to return defective goods, before the maintenance period kicks in. Second, there is an increasing trend to minimize warranty issues in favor of a more robust indemnity clause.

For example, a warranty that the technology does not infringe the rights of any third party is probably less important than an indemnity stating that the indemnitor will indemnify the other party (generally the licensee) and its employees and related parties in the event that the technology infringes the rights of a third party. Third, parties with leverage generally try to restrict warranties to almost nothing, such as *as-is* warranties, and it is customary in the United States to disclaim all implied warranties. Nonetheless, my basic view is that product warranties should generally state that the goods or technology will function substantially in accordance with their documentation and specifications. Service warranties should state that the services will be performed in workmanlike fashion and meet standards that are acceptable in the industry. These are baseline warranties that licensors should be willing to give in the ordinary course.

Licensees may attempt to obtain from licensors a warranty that the software being licensed does not contain "harmful code" such as computer viruses, worms, trap doors, time bombs, undocumented passwords, disabling code (which renders software unusable until a patch or new password is provided), or any similar mechanism or device. If I am representing the licensor, I generally try to make this a qualified "to the best of licensor's knowledge" warranty.

Another warranty issue concerns the various components of a licensed software program. The licensor may be licensing to the licensee a composite product, consisting of components from various sources (and perhaps some open source components), the latter generally referred to as "third party software." The well-represented licensee will strive to have the third party software identified, and to have warranties that have been granted to the licensor pass through to the licensee, so that the licensee will have recourse in the event that some portion of the software does not work as promised. The software license and service agreement attached hereto as Appendix A has reasonable pass-through warranties for the licensee in Section 11(d).

In international licensing, statutes may prescribe what warranties must be given to the licensee. For example, in a number of civil law countries, such as Mexico and France, there is a warranty that the product will have no hidden defects, and this cannot be disclaimed. In general, the laws of many countries do not permit users to disclaim implied warranties. In Brazil, a technical validity period must be stated by the licensor, during which the software program will be supported, which the knowledgeable draftsman can make coterminous with the warranty period.[6]

Limitation of Liability

This is a very important clause, because it states how much liability each party may face beyond the payments due under the contract. Generally speaking, a licensor offering very inexpensive software or technology that is not mission-critical does not wish to be exposed to millions of dollars of potential liability because of some third party infringement claim. On the other hand, a licensee will take the justifiable position that it is in no position to evaluate whether the technology it is licensing from the licensor infringes someone else's rights or not (or whether content it is licensing infringes a third party's copyright), and the licensor should take this risk.
Generally, the clause offers various limits of liability, one for most inter-party breaches, and a higher limitation of liability threshold (or no limitation at all) for such issues as infringement liability and breach of confidentiality. Licensors often try to extend the higher or unlimited liability basket to cover other causes of action, such as breach of warranty by the licensee, the licensee's exceeding the scope of the license, and/or injury to persons and property committed by agents/employees of the other party.

---

[6] Software Law of Brazil, Law No. 9.609 (1998).

A related issue is the exclusion of consequential and other categories of special damages from liability limits. Sometimes the more serious liability issues covered in the preceding sentence are not limited to direct damages, and sometimes they are. It is again a matter of party leverage in most cases. In general, the limitation of liability section should exclude consequential damages, except possibly in the context of infringement, breach of confidentiality, and injury to persons and property. For a fuller discussion of the different categories of damages, please see Appendix C attached hereto, "Key Technology Licensing Terms," which contains a good discussion of the issue.

From the licensor's perspective, it is important that liability not be limited to amounts paid under the agreement, as that could be interpreted to mean that once the licensee has paid the contract amount, it would face no further liability, regardless of its bad acts and the injury it may have caused to the licensor. Therefore, any such liability clause should cap liability to a stated amount, in addition to amounts due under the contract. From the licensee perspective, no cap on the limitation of liability may be desirable, as typically the only licensee obligation is to pay, whereas the licensor is the much more likely party to face substantial risk in an uncapped (or high-capped) liability scenario, particularly relating to infringement of third-party rights.

Exclusion or limitation of liability may not be permitted under the laws of other countries. However, in many countries, the concept of damages is more akin to direct damages in the United States, and generally, consequential or indirect damages would not be permitted in any event. In most civil law countries, liability is for direct and immediate consequences of an act or omission, plus in rare cases, moral (punitive) damages. In addition, individual consumers receive protection under the laws of many countries, and therefore, exclusion of liability by a licensor in a contract with a consumer licensee may be without legal effect.

Indemnity

The indemnity section is very important. Generally, this section is closely related to the limitation of liability section and to the insurance requirements, although few counsel take the time to figure out to what extent indemnity requirements will be covered by insurance. It is customary that matters subject to higher limits, or unlimited liability, under the limitation of liability section will also be subject to indemnity. When I represent the licensor in a transaction, I try to ensure that only third party infringement claims arising in the United States (and perhaps a few other countries) are indemnified, although injuries to persons and property caused by the employees/agents of one party on the premises of the other may also be the subject of an indemnity, and should also be covered by insurance. The licensee's counsel generally will try to expand any geographic limitations on the indemnity.

Assignment

This clause generally appears in the final miscellaneous boilerplate section of the contract, and for this reason, it is too often overlooked in the contract negotiators. However, for a startup company, or indeed for most companies in the fast-moving technology and Internet sector, freedom from restrictions on assignment is crucially important. Generally, assignment clauses try to restrict the ability of the party with less leverage in the agreement from assigning any obligations under the agreement. What this means, whether implicitly or explicitly, is that at least one party will not be able to be acquired by another entity, or sell off a large unit or substantial assets, without the consent of the other party. This is usually too substantial a constraint on the ability of companies in the technology sector to develop naturally and decide when to be acquired or when to sell off a unit or assets, and in the absence of extenuating circumstances, I generally fight overarching constraints on the ability of my client to be acquired. Often one finds that one party is worried that the other party might be purchased by a competitor. In this case, rather than a blanket prohibition on assignment, it makes more sense to require a consent only in the event of acquisition by a direct competitor. Section 13(a) of the software license and service agreement attached hereto as Appendix A is a good example of a reasonably flexible and mutual assignment clause, which permits assignment of obligations in the event of certain major events in the life of either company.

Support/Maintenance

Many support and maintenance issues are covered under "Licensing Models" below. As mentioned, software licensees generally require support, and licensors often see support as an important profit center. Support agreements, which may form part of a license agreement or may be separate, are often billed annually (or sometimes quarterly) in advance as a percentage of the license fee paid by the licensee. It is very common for support payments to be pegged at 15 to 20 percent (sometimes up to 25 percent) of license fees paid (in a traditional license scenario, not subscription service where payments are intended to include both use of the technology and support), although the support percentage or payment amount often is heavily negotiated. A key issue in negotiation of support is generally about problem or bug escalation, involving (1) how quickly will a licensor respond to notice of a software problem, and (2) how quickly will the licensor resolve the problem or bug. The severity of the problem is usually broken into a number of categories or tiers, generally three or four tiers, with Category 1 (or Severity 1) faults or bugs generally being the most serious problems, such as complete system failure, requiring the most urgent response, and Category 4 (or Severity 4) faults or bugs often constituting just minor irritants that can be corrected with the next scheduled release of the licensor's software. A sample escalation clause is found in the agreement attached hereto as Appendix A, in its Exhibit B. Powerful licensees try to include penalty provisions to punish the licensor should the licensor fail to respond to and resolve problems in accordance with the agreed escalation schedule.

Another major support related issue is how many prior versions of software will be supported by a licensor. Licensees with bargaining power often seek to ensure that the licensor will continue to support various prior releases of the software, so that the licensee is under no obligation to upgrade its entire network with a new release or upgrade that may wreak havoc with its network, or may require a licensee to upgrade an operating system (or even hardware) in order to install the upgrade. However, from the licensor perspective, it is very costly to have to support obsolete versions of the software, especially as the number of users of such versions dwindle. It is important for the licensor to ensure that licensees install new versions of the software relatively quickly after release, so that the licensor can avoid supporting versions that are increasingly obsolete. A rule of thumb is that licensors should expect to support any version of software released in the past year (and sometimes longer), and at least the prior version of the software (and often the prior two versions).

Audit

If one party is to pay royalties or commissions to the other party, then the recipient party must have a strong audit right, with penalties for failure to have paid the other party amounts that exceed a certain threshold (e.g., if the paying party has failed to pay more than 5 or 10 percent of the amounts that should have been paid during the period that has been audited). In the event of failure to pay the stated threshold, the costs of the audit are often borne by the audited party. Therefore, the importance of this provision to the recipient of royalties or payments should not be underestimated. The audit notice should specify the time period of the records to be audited (e.g., 2002-2003 sales), and the audit provision should give the auditing persons the right to copy relevant records or portions thereof, or the audit exercise may be futile. Some advance notice that an audit will occur is generally required. One week's notice is fairly standard and should be adequate. Generally, the audit provision also states who can conduct the audit. If a party must use an outside auditor, the audit may be an expensive undertaking. Section 13(d) of the software license agreement attached hereto as Appendix A is a reasonable audit provision.

Licensing Models

For reasons already explained, technology owners prefer a licensing model to a sales model, so that they retain their ownership and control over their intellectual property. Of course, there are a variety of license models. Traditional technology licensing to end users followed the *shrink-wrap* format, where the end user was deemed subject to the end user license agreement upon opening the software package. Such licenses generally have such customary restrictions on the end user as prohibiting the duplication of the licensed technology, the decompilation or reverse engineering of the technology, as well as assignment of the license. Although such licenses were and continue to be somewhat controversial, because they are contracts of adhesion where the end user typically has no opportunity to bargain for the best deal, they have been upheld by most courts around the world when their validity has been challenged. In the online world, the shrink-wrap license generally has been replaced by the click-wrap license, a relatively confusing term which generally means that before an online user can access or download technology, the user must click "I agree" after scrolling though an online set of terms and conditions. This has the merit of requiring a more agreement-related affirmation than breaking open a package under the shrink-wrap scenario. For an example of a click-wrap terms of use or license in the very popular area of video upload services, please see Appendix B attached hereto; the first paragraph indicates how the user assents to the license.

Many companies have moved a step further from traditional software distribution, even distribution over the Internet, toward hosted models of software distribution. Under the hosted models, sometimes called the ASP (applications service provider) model, or software-as-a-service model, there is generally no download of software required. The user merely accesses the desired program on the licensor's servers and never actually installs the licensor's technology on his or her desktop or laptop computer. In the vast majority of cases, the licensor has outsourced the hosting function to a third party telecom or data center or hosting company. This has further advantages for both licensors and licensees. First, virtually no memory or disk space is used on the user's computer, and updates and upgrades take place automatically and do not have to be implemented across a licensee network. Second, many of the licensor's concerns about software theft, piracy, and unauthorized modification or transfer are eliminated. Third, from both the licensor and licensee perspectives, the system is very scalable; the incremental cost of an additional user, other than possibly requiring the licensor to obtain more robust server capacity, is practically nil. Finally, the hosted model increasingly is done on a subscription payment model, often on an annual basis, and licensors are assured an ongoing revenue stream, rather than just earning most revenue, other than maintenance revenue, on the initial technology license/sale. A subscription service payment model can be found in the software license and service agreement attached hereto as Appendix A.

An advantage of the license model, as opposed to the sales model, is that a license model often means that the user will have access to constantly updated technology, which generally means errors are corrected, and to upgraded technology, which generally means that new or better functionality is added. Closely related to this concept is that the user obtains maintenance and support for some period of time, often over the life of the contract. Of course, this relationship entails ongoing cost to the licensee, which may not need much support after the first year.

There are different considerations for the lawyer that derive from whether the client is: (i) a licensee who is licensing content or technology from a licensor, (ii) a technology licensor or content provider, or (iii) developing technology or content or a Web site for the licensee. One of my first questions for the client is: who has the leverage in this deal? Do you need them more than they need you? How important is this deal to your company? Is walking away from the deal, perhaps only temporarily, an option? I tend to ask the client to give me his or her "take" on the deal, ideally even before I have digested the documentation. What is unusual about this deal? What does he or she see as the deal killers at this point? As mentioned, I have one client, a provider of high-end audio technology, who will walk away from any deal in which this technology provider is expected to agree to unlimited liability. The pricing model, according to this client, does not permit the client to accept unlimited liability. A much different pricing model might justify a higher liability limit. My position as an adviser is dictated to a significant extent by which side I'm on: if I'm representing a technology or Web site developer, I will want to secure freedom of action in future deals. This can be an uphill battle, because from the perspective of the technology licensee or recipient, the developer has been paid in full for its development efforts, so all of the work product should be *work-made-for-hire* under copyright principles--that is, it was commissioned by the licensee, and ownership should vest in the licensee.

But this answer is often too easy, too pat. The reason that the licensee contracted with this technology or Web site developer in the first instance probably had much to do with this provider's expertise and experience, perhaps in the very sector of the licensee's business. The licensee would not be likely to contract with someone who had never done development work in this area before. If much of the development relates to what the developer has done before, then the work product created in this deal will resemble, at least in part, the work product created for the last licensee and the next licensee. It seems unfair that the licensee, which may be paying $200 per hour or some other development fee, would believe that it can claim ownership over all of the knowledge embodied in the work product. This position in effect could put the developer out of business in the developer's area of expertise. So even if the licensee owns the work product, the developer must be free to develop something similar in his or her area of expertise in the future. This can take the form of a no-action agreement-an agreement by the licensee to take no action against future development done by the developer for similar development work. Or it can take the form of a license-back to the developer of all or part of the work product. Or even better, some of the development should be carved out of the work product as preexisting work or property of the developer.

Sometimes, the issue is that someone has to develop calls or APIs (applications programming interfaces) to ensure that two products work together. If one party gets ownership of these fairly standard modules, then the other party may have difficulty using the APIs in future development or in future relationships. Working out reasonable ownership and cross-license provisions that enable one party to reap the benefit of the development it commissioned while permitting the other party the freedom to continue offering its services to other parties may require some licensing creativity. Maybe the developer only needs a license-back of technology that is of generic use, not any development that is specific to (or only useable by) a particular licensee.

In addition, whether I am on the licensor or licensee side of a transaction tends to influence the position I will take on issues like warranty, limitation of liability, and indemnity. The licensor generally will want to limit infringement liability; the licensee will want to leave it unlimited. The licensee will want its money back if it cannot use part of the software because it infringes the rights of a third party. The licensor will try to limit the remedy to replace or modify the software to make it non-infringing, and only when this fails will the licensee be reimbursed the prorated, depreciated value of the software modules that were found to be infringing.

Support and Maintenance

Generally, support is available for a technology licensee. The reason is fairly obvious; the licensee generally is not the best positioned party to deal with technical problems as they arise. In a development deal, support by the licensor generally begins after the licensee accepts the technology. In some deals, support will begin after the warranty period has expired; such period may be thirty days or ninety days or a year in duration. More typically, the warranty covers the right to obtain a replacement during some initial period, but support runs concurrently, and covers various bug fixes and error corrections, and depending on the level of support, improvements or enhancement in functionality as well.

If the traditional license model has been superseded by a subscription services model, the subscription fee, generally paid annually or quarterly (or monthly) in advance, typically will cover support. If a customer wants premium support, whether that means twenty-four/seven support or telephonic support in addition to e-mail or Web support, this might entail an additional payment. Often parties debate how support will be delivered (on-site support is more costly than telephone support, which in turn is more costly than e-mail support), and during what hours, e.g., business hours or around the clock. The traditional support model for technology licenses involves an annual payment in advance, generally on the effective date of a license deal, and then on each anniversary of the effective date. Often a licensee is permitted to discontinue support, sometimes after the first year, sometimes after a few years. Generally, if the licensee discontinues support and then wants to reinstate it, there is a penalty assessed involving payment of all support that would have been due during the gap period, plus an additional penalty amount. Content licensees may not require support, as what is being licensed by nature may not need much attention after the initial content license.

Preparation of the Good Licensing Lawyer

It is my experience that working with a knowledgeable attorney on the other side of a transaction tends to make the transaction move forward smoothly and results in a reasonable deal for both parties. The attorney understands all the issues and probably has represented both licensors and licensees. Working with an attorney who is relatively new to licensing, or who questions all acquired learning on the subject, such as; "Why shouldn't you indemnify against all breaches, not just third party claims?" tends to lead to a long and arduous negotiation, unless the inadequate attorney's client intervenes to get the deal done. In fact, my goal in bad attorney situations is to try to ensure that the businesspeople (especially from the opposing side) are on the call or present at the negotiation, because this may be the only way the deal will get done relatively quickly.

One way I keep mentally fit as an attorney is that sometimes I represent the party in a transaction that lacks leverage, such as a start-up whose technology is not yet widely adopted, and which needs a few marquee clients. This always takes mental agility and creativity to reach a fair deal. A related truth is that I've seen a lot of bad lawyering in companies that have powerful leverage, thereby reducing the attorney's need to think of creative solutions, and allowing the attorney to grow intellectually lazy. This applies in equal measure to high leverage institutions such as banks, governmental entities, and sometimes to large well-known technology companies.

IP licensing is a form of transactional practice and therefore a good background in corporate law is very useful in the formation of a good licensing lawyer. The securities aspects of corporate practice do not tend to be important in IP licensing, but the art of the deal is very important. In addition, a solid background in the various components of intellectual property law, including copyright, trademark, patent and trade secret law, will very much enhance the quality of IP licensing counseling and drafting. Finally, as in many areas of practice, good writing enhances the quality of licensing contracts.

Inadequate attorneys are often unreasonable on acceptance and ownership issues because they lack a sophisticated understanding of such issues as revenue recognition implications. Some attorneys fail to understand that a technology developer must continue offering similar services after this deal is done. They fight over warranties that are standard in the industry. They may fight over limitations of liability and indemnity issues, on the licensee side, trying to expand the indemnity far beyond third party claims and confidentiality breaches, or failing to understand that an indemnity is not the usual remedy for inter-party claims (a breach of contract action under the contract is the ordinary course remedy), and are generally intended to make the more innocent party whole against unanticipated third party claims.

Inadequate attorneys on the other side of a transaction from a start-up company may fail to understand the start-up company mentality. For example, such a lawyer may not grasp that a start-up company and its investors do not plan to allow the other party to a license deal to have the right to consent to a sale of the start-up company. The appropriate remedy in this situation is to give the non-selling party a remedy such as the requirement of consent only if the start-up company would end up in hands that are directly competitive to the non-selling party in the transaction.

Legal vs. Business Decisions

It is generally not the lawyer's function to determine what will trigger payment, as revenue generating decisions are usually dictated by the businesspeople in an organization. Nonetheless, the lawyer can play an important role, by raising "what if" or non-obvious issues, such as should affiliates (generally entities controlling, controlled by, or under common control with the organization entering into the license) have the same rights and terms as the licensee organization? What if the licensee acquires several more companies, will the revenue model be appropriately scalable, or will the payment provisions have to be renegotiated? This may lead into tangential discussions, such as what if a competitor of licensor acquires the licensee? What if the licensee has a license under the licensor's pending patent application, and the patent is not issued? Should the royalty obligation end?

I have licensor clients that bill on a per user basis, or various permutations of this. An example of this is online banking security software that bills its financial institution customers based on the number of users of their product. Billing may be based on tiers of usage, rather than individual usage, as indicated in the software license agreement attached hereto as Appendix A. Other clients bill based on instances of use of a given product, or on number of concurrent users on a network, or on number of named users, or on number of seats or devices that use a given program or product. I have several software company clients that bill customers based on CPU processing capacity (the higher the processing capacity, the higher the payment), which is fairly common in the work station and mainframe software worlds. The advantage of billing on a scalable method is that as an enterprise grows, there is no need to renegotiate the license agreement, as the payment amounts that are due will automatically adjust. Notwithstanding these methods, much enterprise software and other software as well is licensed on an enterprise-wide basis or site license, meaning that there may be a fixed payment, or fixed annual payment, regardless of the volume of use.

It is helpful for the licensing lawyer to keep abreast of revenue recognition guidelines, because this is very useful to clients. While these provisions are complex, generally licensors cannot recognize revenue until acceptance has occurred when there are acceptance criteria. It is also the case that support payments, even when made in advance as is the custom, must be recognized over the term of the support agreement, rather than at the time of payment.

Characteristics of Different Licensing Models

As mentioned above, many companies have moved from packaged software distribution models to software download models, and recently to software-as-a-service or ASP hosted models. Among the most innovative companies in this space is salesforce.com, which has a renowned set of software services that help companies run, all accessible online. Many other companies have followed suit. While I often discuss the benefits and pitfalls of such a paradigm change with my client, it is generally the client, and not the lawyer, that chooses when to make the shift to a subscription-based services model from a license-based package distribution or download model.

There are a number of advantages to the subscription model. Although less revenue is generally recognized up front as in the case of a license, there is the prospect of a multi-year recurring revenue stream, rather than a one-time license payment "spike." This helps improve long-term prospects for technology companies. In addition, there is virtually no piracy problem, as applications are generally run on host company servers, rather than existing on the hard drives or servers of the client. As additional users are added, there are virtually no incremental costs to be incurred by the licensor, other than to increase server capacity from time to time.

Issues such as the scope of a license are often heavily negotiated. Is the license perpetual, or is it for a particular term? Generally, end users have the expectation that they can use technology subject to license for as long as the technology is viable, although this is changing as the time-limited hosted subscription or software-as-a-service model grows in popularity. Is the license irrevocable, or is it terminable by the licensor? Is it royalty free? Most licenses generally require at least an initial payment. Can the licensed technology be modified by the user? Can the licensed technology be transferred by the user? Who owns modifications made by the user?

Many provisions of licenses turn on whether it is an intermediary who is licensed or given rights to use, modify, and/or resell a product, or an end user. For example, if one technology company licenses in a third-party software product and combines that product with its own product, and then offers its own product plus the other product to customers, that intermediary may be called an OEM, a VAR, or even, depending on the role of the reseller, a systems integrator. [7]

Because the intermediary may have rights to modify the product, or at least to develop interfaces, often called APIs, to connect several products, the intermediary is often subject to a term of limited duration and ongoing payment obligations. On the other hand, end users who have only the right to use a product, and not to resell it (even if they have modification rights), do not tend to have their use limited in time, unless they are on a subscription basis. Payments under a license are generally called royalties. A royalty is the sum of money paid to the owner or licensor of intellectual property rights for the benefits derived, or sought to be derived, by the user (the licensee) through the exercise of such rights. Royalties are often calculated as a percentage, such as a percentage of the license/sales price of a technology or entertainment product, a percentage of aggregate revenues received from end users (less items such as taxes and returns), or a stated percentage of SRP, or suggested retail price. If a reseller is combining several products, the royalty back to the licensor for one of the products may be an estimate of the value that such product bears to the overall combined product sales price. A royalty is sometimes called a commission. Some countries apply withholding taxes to royalty transfers to a foreign licensor, but not to sales price remittances. In

---

[7] OEM means Original Equipment Manufacturer, and derives from when a hardware manufacturer would offer third party software with its hardware. Now it is frequently one software company licensing in the product of another software company. VAR means Value Added Reseller. A VAR offers for license at least two products from different sources, whether both are third party products, or one is the VAR's product.

such cases, parties go to extraordinary lengths to try not to characterize payments as a royalty. This may be more convincing if, for example, the transaction involves the distribution of mass market software, in which the user acquires the product, technically under license, but does not customize the product and can use it indefinitely. This license is very much like a product sale, and the payments may not be characterized as royalties. Determining royalty rates, just as determining how to sell a product, is generally a business decision. There are certain customs in the technology industry, such as annual support and maintenance payments, being calculated as a percentage of the overall license price, often from 15 to 25 percent of the license price, with payment either annually or quarterly in advance. This is changing, however, as parties move to a subscription services model, in which support costs are folded into the annual charges for use of, or access to, a technology product.

Laws Relevant to Licensing

First, most intellectual property licenses involve, to some extent, copyright law for content and software, patent law, and trademark law, all of it largely governed by federal law in the United States. The concept of many licenses is to augment the control of the licensor beyond mere reliance on copyright law to ensure that the buyer or licensee of a product is restricted in the disposition of the licensed products and will not make copies (or more than the stated number of copies). Because under copyright principles, once a copyrighted product is sold into commerce, the buyer can resell the product without restriction; it is the license that often over-rides this first sale doctrine.

If content is made available on a Web site, and a third party claims ownership of such content, it is again copyright law, particularly the Digital Millennium Copyright Act (DMCA), that may insulate the Web site owner from liability because of its safe harbor exceptions to copyright liability. This is a copyright law reform that provides a notice-and-takedown procedure which, if followed by the Web site owner, may protect such owner from infringement claims. These laws are the basic building blocks for a good licensing lawyer. Note that in Appendix B, the online service provider's language under "Use of Web VideoVillages…" is intended to ensure that the Web site falls within one of the DMCA safe harbors from infringement liability.

Other laws that affect the exhibition of content, such as the Communications Decency Act and various privacy related laws such as the Children's Online Privacy Protection Act, are also federal. The latter law applies to Web sites or online services directed at children under thirteen that collect personal information from children, or general audience Web sites with actual knowledge that personal information is being collected from children. Related to protection of intellectual property, especially in the world of content, may be privacy laws that protect personally identifiable information from disclosure. While the United States generally has lagged Europe, Canada, Australia, and other countries in giving strong protection to personally identifiable data about individuals, outside certain contexts such as health and banking, this may be changing. There is bipartisan support in Congress for more robust protection of the handling, use, and security of personal data, so this area which had largely been left to the states in the United States may soon be federalized.

State laws do not tend to be as central to licensing, with the exception of trade secret laws. When licensing something that is the subject of trade secret protection, the licensor must ensure that the licensee is required by contract to take great care to preserve the confidentiality of the trade secret information, in accordance with applicable state law. In addition, most privacy laws in the United States are state laws, but there is considerable support in Congress for stronger federal laws which would preempt much of the state legislation.

Richard E. Neff is a partner at Greenberg Glusker, a Los Angeles-based law firm, where he heads the Intellectual Property and Technology Department He specializes in complex transactions and licensing deals involving intellectual property for a broad range of clients including many technology and Internet companies, and in anti-piracy issues. Often his transactions have international aspects. From 1992 to 2004, he was the senior partner of Neff Law Group, a law firm that handled technology transactions and anti-piracy enforcement for a renowned international client base. He represents or has represented such companies as Logitech, Symantec, Intuit, Microsoft, Autodesk, Apple, SunGard Data Systems, Yahoo!, Business Software Alliance (BSA), Informatica, RSA Security and PriceGrabber.com. Prior to that, he was Deputy General Counsel, International for Ashton-Tate Corp., the publisher of the dBASE family of software, and was a founder and chairman of the BSA. He writes frequently on intellectual property issues, and previously co-authored a book entitled NAFTA: Protecting and Enforcing

Intellectual Property Rights in North America, *which was published by Shepard's McGraw Hill. Mr. Neff has a B.A. from Cornell University with distinction in all subjects, a J.D. from Yale Law School, where he was an editor of the Yale Law Journal (1979 to 1980), and he was a Fulbright Scholar in Lima, Peru from 1976 to 1977.*

About Greenberg Glusker Fields Claman & Machtinger LLP

Greenberg Glusker, a full service business and entertainment law firm based in Los Angeles, provides the highest quality legal services and strategic business advice to companies and individuals. We are a multi-specialty Firm where experienced practitioners work together as a team across disciplinary lines to solve legal problems. Our areas of practice include: Litigation, Real Estate, Land Use, Environmental, Entertainment, Intellectual Property and Technology, Business and Tax, Labor and Employment, Estate Planning, and International Transactions. In June 2007, Los Angeles Daily Journal *selected Greenberg Glusker as one of the top three entertainment practices in Southern California.*

The historic strength of its media-focused entertainment transactional and litigation practices spurred the Firm to expand the Intellectual Property and Technology practice group, so that the Firm would be at the forefront of the convergence between media and technology, of which Southern California may be the epicenter. In addition to a very strong practice focused on branding (trademarks, service marks, domain names) and copyright, Greenberg Glusker has developed renowned expertise in Internet and technology issues. The IP and Technology Dept. focuses upon the protection and commercialization of valuable intellectual property assets and enforcement of related rights around the world, working on interesting media and licensing issues with the Entertainment, Litigation and Business and Tax departments, depending upon the nature of a particular transaction or claim.

Dedication: *To my parents and brothers, and my children, Josh, Sara, and Hilary.*

APPENDIX A

SOFTWARE LICENSE AND SERVICE AGREEMENT

[Prepared for the Licensor]

This Software License And Service Agreement (the "Agreement") is entered into by and between Licensor, a [STATE] corporation ("LICENSOR"), with principal offices at 1900 Avenue of the Stars, Los Angeles, CA 90067, USA and [CUSTOMER NAME], a [STATE] corporation ("LICENSEE"), with principal offices at 1600 Pennsylvania Avenue, NW, Washington, DC 20004, USA, as of the Effective Date.

The Agreement sets forth the terms and conditions under which LICENSOR will license to LICENSEE its Licensed Software program to perform the Services (as defined below).

1.   Definitions. The following definitions shall be used for purposes of this Agreement.

a.   "Effective Date" means _____, 20__.

b.   "Error" means a material failure of the Licensed Software to conform to its functional specifications, which failure is demonstrable on LICENSEE's computer or server and which material failure causes the Licensed Software to be inoperable, to operate improperly, or to produce results materially different from those described in any written specifications supplied to LICENSEE. Failures resulting from the following are not Errors: (i) LICENSEE's negligence or improper use of the Licensed Software, or (ii) LICENSEE's use of the Licensed Software in combination with any third party database or other software not identified as compatible by LICENSOR.

c.   "Licensed Software" means (a) the Licensed Software developed by LICENSOR described on Exhibit A hereto, in its standard object code form as made generally available to all licensees during the Term and any component thereof, and (b) any customizations which LICENSOR may create specifically for LICENSEE during the Term; including computer software (in object code form only), algorithms, data, content, and documentation (in electronic form only) that LICENSOR has developed or may develop during the Term and any component thereof. The Licensed Software shall not include products, functionality or code which (a) is specifically developed on a customized basis for another party other than LICENSEE, or (b) is outside the scope of the Services.

d. "Licensed Software User" means a customer of LICENSEE with whom LICENSEE utilizes any portion of the Licensed Software to perform the Services.

e. "Production Notice" means a written notice given to LICENSOR by LICENSEE within thirty (30) days to LICENSEE's intended production use of the Licensed Software. The Production Notice constitutes acceptance of the Licensed Software.

f. "Services" means [DESCRIBE THE SERVICES]

2. <u>Term</u>. The "Term" of this Agreement is five (5) years, which shall commence on the Effective Date and shall end on the fifth anniversary of the Production Notice unless sooner terminated by a party hereto in accordance with this Agreement.

3. <u>License</u>.

a. <u>Software License Grant</u>. During the Term, LICENSOR hereby grants LICENSEE a non-exclusive, nontransferable license to run and use the Licensed Software as listed in Exhibit A, and any updates thereto, on computers owned or controlled by LICENSEE in accordance with related documentation only for LICENSEE's own use in providing the Services.

b.   <u>Copies and Adaptations.</u>

(1)   LICENSEE may copy the Licensed Software provided by LICENSOR in machine readable form and make sufficient copies thereof if necessary for LICENSEE's own use and for backup and archival purposes, provided that LICENSEE shall not make more copies than the minimum it needs for these purposes.

(2)   LICENSOR is not responsible for any merges or adaptations of the Licensed Software done by or for LICENSEE, or the compatibility of any software, hardware, or service with such adaptations. LICENSEE shall pay LICENSOR for services necessitated by adaptations of any of the Licensed Software or by LICENSEE's failure to use current software and releases provided by LICENSOR at LICENSOR's standard consulting rates on a time and materials basis.

(3)   LICENSEE shall reproduce and include LICENSOR's copyright and/or trade secret notices on all copies and adaptations in any form of the Licensed Software.

c.   <u>Trademark and Marketing Licenses</u>. Each party's use of the other party's trademarks will conform at all times with the owning party's quality and usage requirements and will be subject to prior review and approval by the owning party. Neither party will seek to register any trademarks of the other party in any country in the world. Any trademark use shall be in accordance with each party's reasonable policies regarding advertising and trademark usage as established from time to time.

d.   <u>Restrictions</u>. LICENSEE will not directly or indirectly (i) reverse assemble, reverse engineer, decompile or otherwise attempt to derive source code from the Licensed Software or any component thereof; (ii) modify, adapt, translate, transform or prepare derivative works of the Licensed Software, (iii) copy, reproduce, rent, modify, sell, lease, lend, transfer, transmit, broadcast, publicly or digitally perform or display, upload or post, convey, assign, sublicense, market, commercially exploit, or otherwise permit access to third parties to, the Licensed Software or any component thereof other than as expressly provided in this Agreement; (iv) use Licensed Software in any manner that infringes the intellectual property or other rights of another party; (v) distribute or re-distribute Licensed Software; or (vi) use the Licensed Software to provide service-bureau, software rental, time sharing or any services to any third party. If LICENSEE is located in the European Union and wishes to decompile the Licensed Software pursuant to the rights accorded under the EC Council Directive 14 May 1991 on the legal protection of software ("the Directive"), LICENSEE must (i) give LICENSOR thirty (30) days' written notice of its intent to decompile the Licensed Software; (ii) permit representatives of LICENSOR to be present for the decompilation, (iii) covenant that no information obtained from such decompilation shall be used in a manner inconsistent with the Directive, and (iv) covenant that no decompilation permitted in accordance with this sentence shall take place nor shall any information obtained from such decompilation be transferred out of the Member States of the European Union.

4.   Delivery and Installation. As soon as practical after the Effective Date, or as soon thereafter as the parties may agree, LICENSOR shall electronically deliver to LICENSEE for its use during the Term of this Agreement, a copy of the Licensed Software programs in machine readable form (object code). Simultaneously with delivery and at LICENSEE's request, LICENSOR shall provide the Standard Implementation and Setup services set out in Exhibit A below (the fee for this implementation, implementation and training service is set out in Exhibit A). Thereafter, LICENSOR will provide professional services to LICENSEE as requested and LICENSEE shall pay (i) a professional services fee for such services at LICENSOR's rate specified on Exhibit A; and (ii) all reasonable out of pocket expenses incurred by LICENSOR, including travel, lodging, and meal expenses.

5.   Support Services and Training. LICENSOR shall provide support services by email or by telephone to LICENSEE's technical personnel to assist in using the Licensed Software, between the hours of 8:00AM and 6:00PM Pacific Time, Monday through Friday, excluding national holidays (collectively "Standard Support Services") and will provide a number for after hours support for emergencies that prevent Licensed Software Users generally from being able to access LICENSEE's on-line applications. The support services provided under this Section 5 shall be as described in the service level description which is attached hereto as Exhibit B and incorporated herein by reference. Should LICENSEE require a higher level of service, such as 24/7 support, LICENSOR shall provide premium support for an additional charge, as stated in Exhibit A.

6.   LICENSEE Responsibilities.

        a.   LICENSEE Responsible for System Requirements. LICENSEE is responsible for obtaining all hardware, software and Internet connections needed to load and use the Licensed Software. All such facilities and services shall comply with LICENSOR's specifications. LICENSOR shall have no responsibility for such hardware, software and Internet connections and LICENSEE's computer systems and networks in general.

        .b.   LICENSEE Responsible for System Integration. LICENSEE is responsible for the integration of the Licensed Software into their computer system applications.

        c.   LICENSEE Responsible for Upgrading Software. LICENSEE is responsible to upgrade the Licensed Software no less frequently than annually. LICENSEE may delay this upgrade only with the signed mutual consent of both parties.

        d.   LICENSEE Responsible for Production Notice. LICENSEE shall submit a Production Notice to LICENSOR, subject to LICENSEE's payment obligations set forth on Exhibit A hereto.

e.   Press Release. LICENSEE and LICENSOR shall jointly issue a press release reasonably acceptable to both parties identifying LICENSOR as providing [NATURE OF SERVICES] services for LICENSEE, and LICENSEE shall make a contact person available for customer and press references during the Term.

7.   Fee Payments; Late Charges.

a.   Fee Payment.

(1)   Licensed Software Fees. During the Term, LICENSEE shall pay LICENSOR the license fees for the Licensed Software set forth on Exhibit A. LICENSEE will be responsible for calculating the number of Active End Users (as defined on Exhibit A), subject to LICENSOR's right to audit. License fees will be due and payable 15 days after the close of each month.

(2)   Professional Service Fees. LICENSOR will periodically bill LICENSEE for professional services or customization services, plus out-of-pocket expenses, on the terms set forth on Exhibit A. Such billings will be due and payable 30 days after the date of each billing.

b.   Late Charges. Any delinquent amount owing shall accrue interest at the rate of one and one-half percent (1.5%) per month or the maximum amount permitted by law, whichever is less.

8.   Taxes. Prices set forth herein are exclusive of all taxes. LICENSEE shall pay (and LICENSOR shall have no liability for), any taxes, tariffs, duties and other charges or assessments imposed or levied by any government or governmental agency in connection with this Agreement, including, without limitation, any federal, provincial, state and local sales, use, goods and services, value-added and personal property taxes on any payments due in connection with the license and services provided hereunder.

9.   Ownership.

a.   LICENSOR. LICENSOR and its licensors shall retain and own all right, title and interest and all intellectual property rights (including but not limited to copyrights, trade secrets, trademarks and patent rights) in and to the Licensed Software and all copies thereof, and nothing herein transfers or conveys to the LICENSEE any ownership right, title or interest in or to the Licensed Software or to any copy thereof or any license right with respect to same not expressly granted herein. The LICENSEE will not, either during or after the termination of this Agreement, contest or challenge the ownership of the intellectual property rights in the Licensed Software.

b.   LICENSOR shall retain and own all right, title and interest and all intellectual property rights (including but not limited to copyrights, trade secrets, trademarks and patent rights) to all information which is collected, submitted to and made available to either party in the course of the performance by either party of their obligations under this Agreement (or where such title cannot be granted or otherwise transferred to LICENSOR then LICENSEE agrees to grant LICENSOR an unconditional, unlimited, unrestricted, royalty free license to use, distribute and/or otherwise make available such information).

c.   Protection of Proprietary Rights. Neither party shall remove any copyright, patent, trademark, design right, trade secret, or any other proprietary rights legends from the information or materials provided by the other party, including, in the case of information and materials provided by Licensor, the Licensed Software.

d.   Indemnification.

(1)   Each party ("indemnifying party"), at its own expense, will defend any action brought by a third party against the other party ("indemnified party") to the extent that it is based on a claim that the Licensed Software, or

any other intellectual property of the indemnifying party, used within the scope of this Agreement, infringes any United States patent, copyright, license, trade secret, or other proprietary right of a third party in the United States, provided that the indemnifying party is immediately notified in writing of such a claim. The indemnifying party shall have the right to control the defense of all such claims, lawsuits, and other proceedings, provided that the indemnified party shall lend all reasonable cooperation and assistance (any assistance in excess of 20 person-hours shall be reasonably compensated by the indemnifying party). In no event shall the indemnified party settle any such claim, lawsuit, or proceeding without the indemnifying party's prior written approval. The indemnifying party shall have no liability for any claim under this Section if a claim for patent, copyright, license, or trade secret infringement is based on the use of a superseded or altered version of the Licensed Software or other information provided, if such infringement would have been avoided by use of the latest unaltered version of the Licensed Product available as an update or upgrade, or by the use of such other information provided.

(2)   The indemnifying party further agrees to indemnify and hold harmless the indemnified party, its agents, employees, successors, and assigns from and against any and all liabilities, losses, damages, claims, suits and expenses, including legal expenses from any and all claims by any third party resulting from the negligence, willful misconduct or misrepresentations of the indemnifying party or its employees, representatives, or agents.

(3)   The indemnifying party's sole obligation, other than the indemnification obligation set forth above, in the event of such a third party infringement claim, is to secure for LICENSEE the right to continue using the Licensed Software or other intellectual property at issue, or to

develop a non-infringing workaround and provide it to the indemnified party. In the event neither result is reasonably practicable, the indemnifying party shall refund to the indemnified party the fees paid by the indemnified party relating to the infringing intellectual property over the previous 12 months

10.   Confidential Information.

a.   Each party acknowledges that confidential information (including trade secrets and confidential technical, financial and business information (collectively, "Confidential Information") may be exchanged between the parties pursuant to this Agreement. In addition, the Licensed Software, related documentation, and this Agreement shall be LICENSOR Confidential Information. The receiving party (the "recipient") shall use no less than the same means it uses to protect its similar confidential and proprietary information, but in any event not less than reasonable means, to prevent the disclosure and to protect the confidentiality of the Confidential Information of the disclosing party (the "disclosing party"). The recipient agrees that it will not disclose or use the Confidential Information of the disclosing party except for the purposes of this Agreement and as authorized herein. The recipient will promptly report to the disclosing party any unauthorized use or disclosure of the disclosing party's Confidential Information that the recipient becomes aware of and provide (at the expense of the disclosing party) reasonable assistance to the disclosing party in the investigation and prosecution of any such unauthorized use or disclosure.

b.   Confidential Information shall not include information that is: (i) already known by the recipient without an obligation of confidentiality, (ii) publicly known or becomes publicly known through no unauthorized act of the recipient, (iii) rightfully received from a third party without any obligation of confidentiality, (iv) independently developed by the recipient without use of the Confidential Information of the disclosing party, (v) approved by the disclosing party for disclosure, or (vi) required to be disclosed pursuant to a subpoena, or requirement of a governmental agency or law so long as the recipient provides the disclosing party with notice prior to any such disclosure to afford the disclosing party the opportunity to oppose disclosure, and takes all reasonable steps to maintain the information in confidence.

c.   LICENSEE also agrees not to use LICENSOR's Confidential Information to create any computer software or documentation that is substantially similar to the Licensed Software.

d.   Notwithstanding anything to the contrary herein, the rights and obligations set forth in this Section, may be enforced by legal action seeking injunctive relief.

11.   Limited Warranty; Disclaimer of Liability.

a.   During the Term, LICENSOR warrants that the Licensed Software will function and process data materially in accordance with its specifications and that any Errors will be corrected in a timely manner using commercially reasonable efforts.

b.   TO THE MAXIMUM EXTENT PERMITTED BY APPLICABLE LAW, LICENSOR DISCLAIMS ALL OTHER REPRESENTATIONS, WARRANTIES, TERMS AND CONDITIONS, WHETHER EXPRESS OR IMPLIED BY STATUTE, COLLATERALLY, THE PARTIES' COURSE OF DEALINGS OR OTHERWISE, REGARDING THE LICENSED SOFTWARE, RELATED DOCUMENTATION OR INFORMATION, AND OTHER MATERIALS AND SERVICES, INCLUDING THEIR FITNESS FOR A PARTICULAR PURPOSE, SATISFACTORY QUALITY, MERCHANTABLE QUALITY, OR NON-INFRINGEMENT. LICENSOR LICENSORS DISCLAIM ALL REPRESENTATIONS, WARRANTIES, TERMS AND CONDITIONS, WHETHER EXPRESS OR IMPLIED BY STATUTE, COLLATERALLY, THE PARTIES' COURSE OF DEALINGS OR OTHERWISE, INCLUDING WITHOUT

LIMITATION, TITLE, FITNESS FOR A PARTICULAR PURPOSE, MERCHANTABILITY AND NON-INFRINGEMENT. LICENSOR does not warrant that the functions contained in the Licensed Software or in any update will meet the requirements of LICENSEE or that the operation of the Licensed Software will be uninterrupted or error free or free from Errors or other program limitations.

c.   Any warranty, term or condition made hereunder is void to the maximum extent permitted under applicable law if (i) the Licensed Software, or any part thereof, has been subject due to the acts or omissions of the LICENSEE to any unauthorized neglect, misuse, movement of location, use of unauthorized software or media, tampering, or any event other than ordinary use; (ii) any copy of the Licensed Software has been altered or changed in any way by LICENSEE, (iii) there have been changes in or modifications to the operating characteristics of any computer hardware or operating system for which the Licensed Software or an update are procured; (iv) problems occur as a result of the use of the Licensed Software in conjunction with non-licensor software not provided by or integrated by LICENSOR or with hardware which is incompatible with the operating system for which the Licensed Software is being procured or (v) LICENSEE is in default of any term or condition of this Agreement.

d.   Any software published by third parties, which is provided under this Agreement is subject to and in accordance with the terms and conditions of the respective standard purchase or license agreements. To the extent that any software licensor has made any assignable warranties or other commitments to LICENSOR, LICENSOR hereby assigns, to the extent permissible, all of the respective warranties and other commitments related to the software, provided that LICENSEE is not in breach of any provision of this Agreement, and except as otherwise expressly set forth above, LICENSOR does not make any warranties with respect to the products of third party software licensors, if any, supplied with the Licensed Software, and LICENSEE agrees to look only to such third party for any warranty claim relating thereto. Notwithstanding any terms of this Agreement to the contrary, additional terms may be added to this Agreement from time to time, upon thirty (30) days' written notice, as may be reasonably required to comply with LICENSOR's requirements. LICENSEE's failure to object to such notice in writing during such 30-day period shall be deemed acceptance of such additional terms. The source code of certain third party software provided to LICENSEE hereunder is available to LICENSEE from LICENSOR, and may be obtained at [GIVE URL]. To the extent the terms of this Agreement differ from the license terms provided to LICENSOR by LICENSOR's licensors, LICENSEE acknowledges that such differing terms in this Agreement are offered solely by LICENSOR and not LICENSOR's licensors.

e.   TO THE MAXIMUM EXTENT PERMITTED BY APPLICABLE LAW, LICENSOR'S SOLE OBLIGATION AND LICENSEE'S SOLE REMEDY FOR ANY FAILURE OF THE LICENSED SOFTWARE IS LIMITED TO THE CORRECTION, ADJUSTMENT OR REPLACEMENT OF LICENSED SOFTWARE WHICH EXAMINATION INDICATES, TO LICENSOR'S SATISFACTION, TO BE DEFECTIVE OR, AT LICENSOR'S OPTION, REMOVAL OF THE LICENSED SOFTWARE AND REFUND OF ANY FEES PAID BY LICENSEE FOR THE FAILED PORTION DURING THE TWELVE (12) MONTHS PRECEDING FAILURE. IN NO EVENT, SHALL LICENSOR AND ITS LICENSORS BE LIABLE FOR INDIRECT, SPECIAL, CONSEQUENTIAL, INCIDENTAL, EXEMPLARY, OR PUNITIVE DAMAGES, PENALTIES, CLAIMS FOR LOST DATA, REVENUE, PROFITS OR BUSINESS OPPORTUNITIES, WHETHER IN CONTRACT OR IN TORT INCLUDING NEGLIGENCE, EVEN IF LICENSOR HAD OR SHOULD HAVE HAD ANY KNOWLEDGE, ACTUAL OR CONSTRUCTIVE, OF THE POSSIBILITY OF SUCH DAMAGES. Nothing in this Agreement shall exclude or limit liability for death or personal injury resulting from the negligence of either party or their servants, agents or employees or for fraudulent misrepresentation or for the breach of confidentiality obligations or of the other party's intellectual property rights as set forth herein.

f.   Both parties acknowledge that the prices set forth herein are determined on the basis of the limitations of liability set out in this Section 11, and any modification in the allocation of risk between the parties, including the disclaimer of representations, warranties, terms, conditions in this Section 11 and the indemnification obligations in Section 9(d), would affect the fees charged by LICENSOR, and in consideration of the fees charged hereunder, LICENSEE agrees to the stated allocation of risk.

12.   Termination.

a.   Events of Termination.

(1)   LICENSOR may terminate this Agreement if LICENSEE fails to make payment when due of any amount which is not subject to a bona fide payment dispute (as substantiated in correspondence between the parties) and LICENSEE fails to cure such default within ten (10) business days of receiving notice in writing of such default.

(2)   Either party may terminate this Agreement effective immediately and without liability, upon written notice to the other party, if the other party becomes the subject of a voluntary or involuntary petition in bankruptcy or any voluntary or involuntary proceeding relating to insolvency, receivership, liquidation, or assignment for the benefit of creditors.

(3)   Either party may terminate this Agreement upon written notice with immediate effect in the event of a material breach of this Agreement by the other party which is not remedied to the reasonable satisfaction of the claiming party within thirty (30) days of such party providing written notice of the breach to the defaulting

party which written notice will provide the defaulting party with sufficient detail to remedy the breach.

b.   Effect of Termination. Expiration of the Term, or termination of the Agreement shall terminate the licenses granted hereby. Except to the extent agreed to in writing by the parties: (i) LICENSEE shall pay forthwith all amounts due and owing under this Agreement on the date of termination; and (ii) within five (5) business days after such termination, LICENSEE will either destroy or return to LICENSOR the originals and all copies of the Licensed Software in its possession or under its control, and an officer of that party shall certify in writing that the party has done so.

c.   Survival. In addition to any other provision in which the parties agree that such provision shall survive termination of the Agreement, the following provisions shall survive termination of this Agreement: Payment Terms; Ownership and Licenses; Confidential Information; Warranty Disclaimer; Limitation of Liability; Termination; and General Provisions.

13.   General Provisions.

a.   Successors and Assigns. This Agreement shall bind and inure to the benefit of each party's permitted successors and assigns. Neither party may assign this Agreement, in whole nor in part, without the other party's prior written consent, which may not be unreasonably withheld. Notwithstanding the foregoing, each party may assign any of its rights or obligations without prior written consent of other party in the event of: (i) a merger, reorganization, consolidation or other transaction in which the shareholders of such party before such transaction own less than fifty percent (50%) of the outstanding voting equity securities of the surviving corporation, (ii) a sale or other transfer of all or substantially all of the assets of such party, (iii) a transfer to an entity controlled by, controlling, or under common control with such party provided that the Licensed Software continues to be used by and for LICENSEE's Licensed Software Users or (iv) a transfer of more than fifty percent (50%) of the outstanding voting equity securities of such party in one transaction or a series of related transactions. Any attempt to assign this Agreement without such consent will be null and void.

b.   Governing Law; Arbitration and Venue. This Agreement shall be governed by and construed in accordance with the state and federal laws applicable in the State of California. All disputes arising out of this Agreement shall be settled by binding arbitration in accordance with the Commercial Arbitration Rules of the American Arbitration Association. The arbitration will be conducted in Los Angeles County, California, and the decision of the arbitrators will be final and may be reduced to judgment in any court of competent jurisdiction.

c.   Attorney Fees. If any dispute arising out of this Agreement or any action or proceeding to enforce a judgment based on a cause of action arising out of this agreement is arbitrated or litigated between the parties hereto, the prevailing party shall be entitled to recover its costs of suit, including reasonable legal fees in addition to any other relief to which it may be entitled. In the event of a default in payment hereunder, the injured party may recover its costs of collection, including but not limited to legal fees.

d.   Audit Right. LICENSOR shall have the right no more than once per year to engage at its own expense (subject to the following provisions), an independent auditor to review the books of LICENSEE to determine the accuracy of the payments made by LICENSEE (and to copy relevant portions thereof), during customary business hours at LICENSEE's or other premises where the relevant books and records may be located. LICENSOR shall give LICENSEE no less than seven (7) days' notice in writing of any such audit. Any shortfall detected, including any interest due thereon, shall be payable to LICENSOR upon demand. In the event that an audit uncovers a shortfall of greater than five percent (5%) for the time period covered by the audit notice, all costs and expenses associated with the audit shall be borne by LICENSEE.

e.   Export Control. This Agreement is subject to restrictions and controls imposed by the laws applicable in the United States laws and regulations relating to exports and to all administrative acts of the US Government pursuant to such laws and regulations. Export, re-export or transshipment of the Licensed Software or any other technical data licensed under this Agreement, or the derivative products thereof, is contingent upon: prior written authorization from LICENSOR; and compliance with all necessary United States Government approvals and licenses.

f.   Force Majeure. With the exception of payment obligations, neither party shall be liable to the other party for any delay or failure in performance if such delay or failure is due to causes beyond its control.

g.   Severability; Waiver; Cumulative Rights and Remedies. If any provision of this Agreement is found invalid or unenforceable, that provision will be enforced to the maximum extent permissible so as to effect the intent of the parties and the remainder of this Agreement will remain in full force and effect. Either party's failure, at any time, to require performance by the other party or to claim a breach of any provision of this Agreement will not be construed as a waiver of any right or remedy accruing hereunder, nor shall any waiver of any breach or obligation constitute a waiver of any subsequent breach or obligation. A waiver of any right accruing to either party pursuant to this Agreement will not be effective unless given in writing. The rights and remedies provided herein are cumulative and not exclusive of any other rights or remedies provided by law or otherwise.

h.   Notices. Any notice, request or other communication required or permitted hereunder shall be in writing and shall be deemed to have been duly given if personally delivered, sent by e-mail, sent by facsimile transmission, or sent by U.S. mail, or express courier to the address shown below, or to such other address as may be designated by a party by giving written notice to the other party pursuant to this section.

LICENSOR
Attention: Vice President & General Counsel
[Name of LICENSOR]
1900 Avenue of the Stars
Los Angeles, CA 90067
Fax No:
Email:

LICENSEE
Attention: Vice President & General Counsel
[Name of Licensee]
1600 Pennsylvania Ave., NW
Washington, DC 20004
Fax No.:
Email:

i.   Relationship of the Parties. The employees of either party shall not be deemed at any time to be employees or servants or agents of the other and each party is and shall remain an independent contractor for all purposes.

j.   Construction; Integration; and Modification. This Agreement will be interpreted fairly in accordance with its terms and without any strict construction in favor of or against either party. This Agreement, including all attachments exhibits and schedules, constitutes the entire agreement between the parties with respect to the subject matter hereof, and supersedes and replaces all prior or contemporaneous understandings or agreements, written or oral, regarding such subject matter. No amendment to or modification of this Agreement will be binding unless in writing and signed by a duly authorized representative of both parties, except as otherwise expressly stated in this Agreement.

k.   Compliance with Law. Each party agrees to comply with all applicable international, national, state, regional and local laws, rules, and regulations in performing its duties hereunder.

l.   <u>Counterparts; Captions</u>. This Agreement may be executed in counterparts, each of which shall be deemed an original, but all of which together shall constitute one and the same instrument. The headings in this Agreement are for the convenience of organization and reference. They are not intended by the parties to have any relevance in the interpretation of this Agreement.

In Witness Whereof, the parties hereto execute this Agreement as of the Effective Date

LICENSOR: LICENSEE:

By: _____   By: _____

Name: _____   Name: _____

Title: _____   Title: _____

Exhibit A

LICENSOR's Licensed Software:

_____

Pricing Table

During the Term, the fees for licensing the Licensed Software shall be the greater of:

(1) $5,000.00 per month or

(2) a fee based on the number of Active End Users, as defined below, who is using the Licensed Software as of the end of each month:

Number of Active End Users	Annual cost per Active End User (in tier)
0 – 100,000	$1.00
100,001- 1,500,00	$0.75
1,500,001 - 3,000,000	$0.50
3,000,001 - 5,000,000	$0.35
5,000,001 +	$0.25

Example 1: 125,000 Active End Users (100,000 x 1.00) + (25,000 x .75) = $118,7500 per year = ($82,500 / 12) = $9,896 per month.

- License Fees are invoiced monthly in arrears and are payable 15 days from the invoice date.
- An "Active End User" means a Licensed Software User who has used the Licensed Software at least once in the course of the 90 days immediately preceding each monthly invoice period.
- An "Agent" is an entity (which may include LICENSOR or third parties) which the LICENSEE may engage to provide the Services to Licensed Software Users using the Licensed Software.
- The LICENSEE will be invoiced based on the aggregate number of Active End Users on record at the end of each billing period.
- Minimum License Fees are $5,000 per month

Standard Implementation and Setup Fee - $25,000 fee plus reasonable travel and living expenses which includes the following:

- Up to three (3) days on-site Standard Implementation and Setup by one LICENSOR representative, performed with the LICENSEE for a single server (redundant or parallel servers count as one server if they expose the same APIs and are otherwise identically configured). Implementation typically covers the following:

  o A kick off meeting used to introduce the team members, define working process, and deliver appropriate documents and software to the customer POC.

- o An onsite technical meeting (typically used for installation support)
- o On site training session used to 'train the trainer' within the LICENSEE's organization
- o On site implementation and integration assistance as needed
- o 100 hours total of phone and e-mail support during Standard Support Services Hours for technical integration questions from a single point of contact
- o LICENSOR work to prepare, configure and deliver the Licensed Software for LICENSEE

The Standard Implementation and Setup Fee will be invoiced to the LICENSEE on the Effective Date.

Professional Services Fees

- Additional Implementation or Training shall be billed at $2,000 per person-day

- Software Customization Services:

LICENSOR's professional services staff is available to work on customizations to facilitate the integration as required. Each project requires a Statement of Work which defines the tasks, deliverables and fees to be paid, followed by Change Orders and ultimately a signed Acceptance document.

Professional Services are quoted at $250 per hour, with a minimum charge for on-site visits of one day.

All fees, rates and minimums above may be increased at LICENSOR's discretion on the first day of the first quarter after each anniversary of the Effective Date by the percentage increase in the CPI-US, All Urban Consumers-All Items, as published for the month immediately preceding the Effective Date and the month immediately preceding each anniversary of Effective Date.

All professional services rates are exclusive of expenses. Travel expenses will include a 10% surcharge to cover arrangement costs.

Premium Support Services Fees

If LICENSEE elects Premium Support Services, then LICENSEE shall be entitled to receive 24/7 technical support services. The annual fees for Premium Support Services are 15 % of the annual subscription fees.

Additional Non-Standard Support Services Hours Fees for Standard Support Services

If LICENSEE elects Standard Support Services, as described in section 5 of this Agreement, and calls technical support during Non-Standard Support Services hours then an additional per-incident support fee will be assessed. The per-incident support cost will be $250/hour with 4 hour minimum per incident during Non-Standard Business Hours.

EXHIBIT B

Support Escalation

1.   ERROR SEVERITY LEVELS

Severity levels are defined by the Error(s) directly resulting from a malfunction of the Licensed Software ("Software") during production use that causes the following conditions at the identified severity levels:

Severity Level	Definition
1	An Error that is a direct result of a malfunction of the Software **causing the Software to be inoperable or substantially unusable** for more than a de minimis number of LICENSEE's end users.
2	An Error that is a direct result of a malfunction of the Software that **causes the Software to function in a limited manner** for more than a de minimis number of LICENSEE's end users.
3	An Error that is the direct result of a malfunction of the Software that results in **loss of minor functionality or performance** that is not evident or disruptive to end users or which impacts a small number of

	LICENSEE's end users. Severity 1 and Severity 2 Errors shall be downgraded to Severity 3 when an acceptable workaround is provided and a permanent solution is not yet available.
4	An Error that is a direct result of a malfunction of the Software that **causes minimal impact to the Software's functionality** and/or minor Errors that **do not impede the operation** of the Software. Includes cosmetic or stylistic issues.

2.   NOTIFICATION AND INCIDENT TRACKING

2.1   LICENSEE shall report Severity 1 and 2 Errors to LICENSOR via telephone. LICENSEE shall report all other Errors to LICENSOR via telephone or email, during normal business hours. LICENSOR will provide the LICENSOR Support telephone number and email to LICENSEE in the Documentation.

2.2   LICENSOR shall assign an Incident Manager to each Severity 1 and 2 Error reported. The Incident Manager shall track the progress of resolution and report status to LICENSEE.

3.   PROVIDING REMEDIES FOR SOFTWARE ERRORS

3.1   LICENSOR Responsibilities

3.1.1   LICENSOR shall work with LICENSEE to understand, quantify and classify the Error and shall attempt to identify, reproduce and validate the Error in a LICENSOR in-house test environment. Ultimately LICENSOR is responsible for determining the Severity Level, but will carefully consider any suggestion of LICENSEE.

3.1.2   LICENSOR shall provide workarounds and/or software fixes, within the Service Level Guidelines, for additional LICENSEE testing and validation. In order to remedy Error(s) LICENSOR shall determine the optimal remedy in its discretion, generally opting for the least invasive remedy, which may include providing LICENSEE with a configuration change, an object code modification (patch release) or a replacement release of the Software.

3.1.3   LICENSOR shall provide LICENSEE with information regarding new releases and associated documentation including a release manifest, deployment and verification instructions.

3.2   LICENSEE's Responsibilities

3.2.1   LICENSEE shall promptly provide LICENSOR with logs, information, and access to system that LICENSOR feels is necessary to diagnose the Error(s).

3.2.2   LICENSEE shall provide required software and related support services (for software other than the Software) to its respective internal resources and/or customers/end users related to the Error (in addition to those support services being delivered by LICENSOR).

3.2.3   LICENSEE shall validate and deploy workarounds and/or fixes to its validation and production environment(s) as provided by LICENSOR.

3.2.4   LICENSEE shall provide support for all non-LICENSOR supported products and infrastructures.

3.2.5   For all Severity 1 & 2 issues, LICENSEE shall identify a single Incident Manager who will be the single point of contact for all incident-related communications. Availability of the Incident Manager throughout the incident resolution period will be required for timely incident resolution.

4. SERVICE LEVEL GUIDELINES

	ERROR Severity 1	ERROR Severity 2	ERROR Severity 3	ERROR Severity 4
Initial Response Time	Within 30 Minutes	Within 2 Business Hours	Next Business Day	N/A
Status Update	Every 2 Hours	Every Day	Weekly	Upon Request
Response Magnitude	Immediate and sustained 24x7 response until system operation is restored.	Takes priority over other scheduled work.	Fixes will be scheduled for next release.	Fixes will be incorporated as engineers perform other updates in the same functional area.
Delivery Method	Workaround or Patch Release	Workaround or Patch Release	Next Scheduled Release	A Scheduled Release

4.1   LICENSOR Service Level Guidelines are in effect during the period from when LICENSOR has assigned the Error a tracking number (which is provided to the LICENSEE reporting the Error) and LICENSOR begins analyzing the Error to identify whether the root cause of the Error is a Software defect until the time when the Error has been fully resolved. Should LICENSOR believe that the Error is not being caused by a Software defect, LICENSOR will still reasonably cooperate with LICENSEE to try to resolve the Error. In the event that LICENSOR believes that the Error is being caused by a Software defect, then the Error is passed to the LICENSOR Software support team to analyze and typically provide a resolution that involves a modification to the Software or its deployment. After the initial response, measurement commences from the time that a tracking number is issued.

APPENDIX B

VIDEOLARK NETWORK USER AGREEMENT

Note: *"VIDEOLARK" is an imaginary video upload service.*

Welcome to VIDEOLARK! We at VIDEOLARK work hard to ensure that you have an enjoyable experience on our web site. Please read this page in its entirety as it explains your rights and responsibilities regarding your use of the VIDEOLARK Network (defined below). You agree to accept the following User Agreement ("Agreement") between you and VideoLark Corporation ("VIDEOLARK"), and your use of the VIDEOLARK Network confirms your acceptance of the terms of this Agreement. In the event that you seek to use portions of the VIDEOLARK NETWORK that require registration, such as our Forums/VideoVillages, our Video Upload Program, and in general any interactive feature of the VIDEOLARK Network, then we will ask during registration that you expressly manifest your acceptance of this Agreement by clicking "I ACCEPT." For purposes of this Agreement, the term "VIDEOLARK Network" means any and all of VIDEOLARK's web sites, including, without limitation, www.videolark.com, as well as any other web sites that may now or hereafter contain an authorized VIDEOLARK-branded area, content, player, or window, provided by VIDEOLARK (collectively, "VIDEOLARK Network")(provided that your use of such VIDEOLARK features on Third Party Web Sites—defined below—may also subject you to the terms of use and privacy policy of such Third Party Web Site).

I.   Subsequent Revisions to Agreement

VIDEOLARK may periodically revise the terms of this Agreement by updating this page. You agree to be bound by subsequent revisions to this Agreement. Accordingly, you should periodically visit this page to review the current terms of this Agreement.

II.   All Rights Reserved

VIDEOLARK reserves all right, title, and interest not expressly granted under this Agreement.

Copyright. All content, which includes, without limitation, articles, films, media files, reviews, software, and source code (collectively, "Content"), on the VIDEOLARK Network is subject to copyright protection and may not be displayed, reproduced, distributed, modified or used in any other manner except with the written permission of VIDEOLARK and its Content providers. The only exception to this may be if a specific item of Content, such as a video that has been submitted to our video upload service, contains express indications that you may make certain use of it because only some rights are reserved to the owner pursuant to a Creative Commons or other limited license.

Trademark. The names or services on the VIDEOLARK Network, including, without limitation, "VIDEOLARK", are trademarks or registered trademarks of VIDEOLARK. Other names or services on the VIDEOLARK Network may be the trademarks of their respective owners. You agree not to use any VIDEOLARK trademarks or any confusingly similar marks for any purpose without the express prior written consent of VIDEOLARK in each instance.

Violations may result in severe civil and criminal penalties.

III.   Use of Material

VIDEOLARK puts valuable Content onto the VIDEOLARK Network, and must carefully protect this Content. VIDEOLARK authorizes you to access and use the Content solely for your personal, non-commercial use, unless a specific item of Content has indications that expressly give you greater rights. You may not sell or modify the Content, and you may not reproduce, republish, upload, display, publicly perform, distribute, or otherwise use the Content in any way for any public or commercial purpose, unless otherwise indicated for a specific VIDEOLARK service or item of Content. You may not use any computerized or automatic mechanism, including without limitation, any web scraper, spider or robot, to access, extract and/or download any Content from the VIDEOLARK Network, unless you are expressly authorized to do so by a specific VIDEOLARK service. As an express condition of your use of the VIDEOLARK Network, you warrant to VIDEOLARK that you will not use the VIDEOLARK Network for any unlawful purpose or purpose prohibited by this Agreement. If you violate any part of this Agreement, your permission to use the Content automatically terminates and you must immediately destroy any copies you have made of any of the Content. The VIDEOLARK Network resides on servers in the United States, and is intended for US users. VIDEOLARK makes no representation that the Content is legal or appropriate for use outside of the United States or that it is authorized for export from the United States or import into any other country. You are solely responsible for complying with all import and export laws and regulations and all applicable laws of any jurisdiction outside of the United States from which you may access the VIDEOLARK Network.

IV.   Your Use of the VIDEOLARK Network

VIDEOLARK tries to maximize user experience on the VIDEOLARK Network, but there are some things that are out of our control, and other things that may go wrong from time to time. The VIDEOLARK Network may contain inaccuracies or typographical errors. VIDEOLARK makes no representations about the accuracy, reliability, completeness, or timeliness of the Content or about the results to be obtained from using the VIDEOLARK Network or the Content. Your use of the VIDEOLARK Network, including, without limitation, the services and information, contained therein, is on an "as is" basis and is at your own risk. VIDEOLARK may make changes in the Content at any time. VIDEOLARK cannot always anticipate technical, access or other difficulties, which may result in loss of Content, data, settings or other service interruptions.

Disclaimer of Liability. VIDEOLARK, ITS RESPECTIVE OFFICERS, DIRECTORS, SHAREHOLDERS, EMPLOYEES, ACCOUNTANTS, ATTORNEYS, AGENTS, AFFILLIATES, SUBSIDIARIES, SUCCESSORS AND ASSIGNS (COLLECTIVELY "VIDEOLARK") SHALL NOT BE LIABLE FOR ANY DIRECT, INCIDENTAL, CONSEQUENTIAL, INDIRECT, OR PUNITIVE DAMAGES ARISING OUT OF OR CONNECTED WITH (I) YOUR USE OF THE VIDEOLARK NETWORK AND (II) ANY OTHER SUBJECT MATTER OF THIS AGREEMENT.

VIDEOLARK Makes No Representations or Warranties. WITHOUT LIMITING THE FOREGOING, EXCEPT AS EXPRESSLY STATED IN THIS AGREEMENT, VIDEOLARK MAKES NO REPRESENTATIONS OR WARRANTIES OF ANY KIND, EITHER EXPRESS OR IMPLIED, AS TO ANY MATTER INCLUDING, WITHOUT LIMITATION, ANY WARRANTY FOR INFORMATION, DATA, SERVICES, OR UNINTERRUPTED ACCESS. SPECIFICALLY, FREIGHT FORCE DISCLAIMS ANY AND ALL WARRANTIES, INCLUDING, BUT NOT LIMITED TO: (1) ANY WARRANTIES CONCERNING THE AVAILABILITY, ACCURACY, USEFULNESS, OR CONTENT OF INFORMATION, OR SERVICES, AND (2) IMPLIED WARRANTIES OF FITNESS FOR A PARTICULAR PURPOSE, MERCHANTABILITY, TITLE, NON-INFRINGEMENT OR OTHERWISE, .

Third Party Links. The VIDEOLARK Network may contain links to web sites operated by parties other than VIDEOLARK ("Third Party Web Sites"), and VIDEOLARK may license Content from the VIDEOLARK Network for use by Third Party Web Sites. VIDEOLARK makes no representation or endorsement of the Third Party Web Sites and you access them at your own risk.

VIDEOLARK Network Modification and Discontinuation. VIDEOLARK reserves the right to modify or discontinue, temporarily or permanently, at any time, any Content or Information (defined below) on the VIDEOLARK Network, or the VIDEOLARK Network itself, or any portion thereof. You agree that any such modification or discontinuation shall be entirely without liability to you or any third party.

Use Of Web VideoVillages and Forums. The VIDEOLARK Network contains forum services, web communities, and other message and communication facilities (collectively, "VideoVillages"), whose use is at your own risk. VIDEOLARK neither endorses nor controls the files, information, or messages (collectively, "Information") delivered to or displayed in the VideoVillages, unless otherwise noted therein, and VIDEOLARK assumes no duty to, and does not, monitor or endorse Information within the VideoVillages, nor does VIDEOLARK represent or guarantee the truthfulness, accuracy or reliability thereof or that the

Information complies with the terms of this Agreement. VIDEOLARK reserves the right at all times, but does not have the obligation, to edit, refuse to post, or to remove any Information, in whole or part, that VIDEOLARK deems inappropriate for inclusion in the VideoVillages, with the goal of ensuring compliance with this Agreement and applicable law. VIDEOLARK reserves the right to expel you from or suspend your access to some or all of the VideoVillages for violating the law or this Agreement. The VideoVillages are public and not private communications and may be read by others without your knowledge or permission. Although a particular Community may have a policy of limited membership or access, VIDEOLARK shall have no liability if unauthorized persons nevertheless obtain access to the Community. Your use of the VideoVillages is at your own risk so be careful about disclosing your personal information.

You should maintain your password (which you will select as part of the process of registration to use interactive portions of the VIDEOLARK Network) in confidence, and not share your password or other access information with any third party. You should notify the VIDEOLARK Network if you need to change your password because its confidentiality has been compromised.

When using the VideoVillages you may not do any of the following:

a. Restrict or inhibit any other user from using and enjoying the VideoVillages;

b. Post or transmit any abusive, hateful, defamatory, indecent, libelous, obscene, pornographic, profane, threatening, harassing, embarrassing, unlawful, vulgar, or other Information of any kind that violates applicable law or regulation or which harms minors in any way, including, without limitation, Information that constitutes the following:

Engage in infringement, i.e., provide or knowingly use Information that violates or infringes upon the copyright, literary, privacy, publicity, trademark, service mark or any other personal or property right of any person or entity or which discloses any trade secret or confidential information.

Upload harmful software, i.e., software or materials that contain a virus, corrupted files, or similar programs that may damage the operation of another's computer or the VIDEOLARK Network.

c.   Post advertisements or solicitations of business, except in areas expressly designated for such purposes and in accordance with the express rules and regulations established by VIDEOLARK.

d.   Post chain letters or pyramid schemes or impersonate another person.

e.   Manipulate headers or identifiers so as to disguise the origin or content of any Information/posting.

f.   Do any act which interferes with or slows the operation of the VIDEOLARK Network.

VIDEOLARK may condition your right to participate in the VideoVillages on your furnishing to VIDEOLARK and keeping updated at all times such personal identifying information as VIDEOLARK may reasonably require, including, without limitation, your true name and a current, active e-mail address. VIDEOLARK reserves the right to suspend or terminate your access to some or all of the VideoVillages if VIDEOLARK has a good faith basis for believing that any of the information you have supplied is inaccurate or that your account is being used by anyone other than you to access the VideoVillages.

By posting Information to the VideoVillages, you automatically grant to VIDEOLARK a royalty-free, perpetual, irrevocable non-exclusive license to use, reproduce, modify, publish, edit, translate, distribute, perform, display and otherwise exploit such Information and all elements thereof alone or as part of other works in any form, media, or technology, whether now known or hereafter developed, and to sublicense such rights through multiple tiers of sublicenses, all without any obligation to you, whether by way of compensation, attribution or otherwise.

V.   VIDEOLARK Network Not for Children

The VIDEOLARK Network is not directed at children under the age of 13. Those portions of the VIDEOLARK Network requiring registration, such as use of VideoVillages, ask that the user's age or birthday be provided, and will automatically exclude from registration those who are under 13. If a person indicates that he/she is under the age of 13, VIDEOLARK shall: not collect the child's personal information; ask the child to provide his/her parent's consent to register with VIDEOLARK; or ask the child to provide a parent's email address so that VIDEOLARK can obtain parental consent to the child's registration with the Web Site, subscription to VIDEOLARK newsletters, and/or participation in other activities and options made available on the Web Site. If a user under the age of 13 wants to participate in online activities offered on the Web Site, we only collect from him/her that information which is reasonably necessary for him/her to participate in the activity. After receipt of a request from a parent, we shall notify the parent what personal information VIDEOLARK has collected from his/her child. Such requests or questions regarding VIDEOLARK's privacy practices should be sent via email to privacy@videolark.com, U.S. mail to VIDEOLARK Corporation, Attn: Privacy Czar, 1900 Avenue of the Stars, Los Angeles, CA 90067.

VI.   Miscellaneous

Privacy. VIDEOLARK's use of personal information you provide or which VIDEOLARK obtains shall be in accordance with VIDEOLARK's privacy policy, as it may be changed from time to time; VIDEOLARK's privacy policy can be found at the bottom of the home page.

Choice of Law and Forum. This Agreement, its interpretation, performance or any breach thereof, will be construed in accordance with, and all questions with respect thereto will be determined by, the laws of the State of California applicable to contracts entered into and wholly to be performed within California. You hereby consent to the personal jurisdiction of the State of California, acknowledge that venue is proper in any state or Federal court in the State of California, agree that any action related to this Agreement must be brought in a state or Federal court in the State of California, and waive any objection you may have in the future with respect to any of the foregoing. Notwithstanding the foregoing, VIDEOLARK reserves the right to commence an action in your home jurisdiction in regards to this Agreement.

Indemnity. You agree to defend, indemnify and hold harmless VIDEOLARK, its licensors, licensees, successors and assignees, its Content providers, advertisers and sponsors, the parent, affiliated and subsidiary companies of each of them and the officers, directors, employees, and agents of each of them from and against any and all third party claims, damages, liabilities, costs and expenses, including reasonable legal fees and expenses, arising out of or related to any breach by you of this Agreement, any material which you may post to the VideoVillages or any use of the Content by you or under your control.

Severability. If any provision of this Agreement, or application thereof, shall be held invalid by a court of competent jurisdiction, such provision shall be changed and interpreted so as to best accomplish the objectives of the original provision to the fullest extent allowed by law and the remaining provisions of this Agreement shall remain in full force and effect.

Use of "You" or "Your". The words "you" or "your" shall also include your heirs, executors, administrators, successors, legal representatives and permitted assigns.

Waiver. Any waiver of any provision of this Agreement must be in writing and signed by an authorized representative of VIDEOLARK.

Copyright Complaints. If you believe that your work or Information has been copied and is accessible on the VIDEOLARK Network in such a manner as to constitute copyright infringement, you may notify VIDEOLARK by providing VIDEOLARK's copyright agent with the following information:

       1.   An electronic or physical signature of the person authorized to act on behalf of the owner of the copyright interest;

2.   A description of the copyrighted work that you claim has been infringed, including the URL (i.e., web page address) of the location where the copyrighted work exists or a copy of the copyrighted work;

3.   Your address, telephone number, and email address;

4.   A statement by you that you have a good faith belief that the disputed use is not authorized by the copyright owner, its agent, or the law; and

5.   A statement by you, made under penalty of perjury, that the above information in your notice is accurate and that you are the copyright owner or authorized to act on the copyright owner's behalf.

VIDEOLARK's agent for notice of claims of copyright infringement on the VIDEOLARK Network may be reached as follows:

>   VIDEOLARK Corporation
>   Attn: Copyright Claims
>   1900 Ave. of the Stars
>   Los Angeles, CA 90067
>   Fax: 888 228 8222
>   copyright@videolark.com

Printed Agreement. A printed version of this Agreement and of any notice given in electronic form shall be admissible in judicial or administrative proceedings based upon or relating to this Agreement to the same extent and subject to the same conditions as other business documents and records originally generated and maintained in printed form.

APPENDIX C

KEY TECHNOLOGY LICENSING TERMS

Why We **License** *Software*
- Software is licensed to define and/or limit user's right to copy and/or modify computer software
- Used to partially avoid reach of copyright law: avoids application of first sale doctrine
- Also permits altering the right of rightful owner to transfer it through rental

What Law Governs Software Contracts
- Art. 2 of the UCC governs transactions involving sale of "goods" in all states except Louisiana
- Courts generally find that software contracts for mass market software (even with some attendant service) are "goods," those calling for substantial service, such as involving development, are not subject to Code
- Issue complicated by "license" rather than "sale" of software; UCC warranty provisions apply to sales, not leases or non-sale transactions
- UCITA in MD, VA—could be enacted elsewhere

Representations vs. Warranties I
- Representation is a statement as to the existence (or not) of a fact or state of affairs or state of mind which acts as inducement to contract
- "Licensor is the owner of the Intellectual Property Rights."
- "To the best of Licensor's knowledge, there has been no infringement of third party rights."
- "There are no liens on the Property."

Representations vs. Warranties II
- Warranty is a guaranty, an assurance of the existence or future existence of a fact upon which the other party may rely

- Currently, an assertion is a representation, and if it will continue into the future, it is a warranty
- "There are no liens on the Property [*representation*] and during the term of the Agreement it shall not become subject to any liens [*warranty*]."

Covenants

- Covenants are simply contractual promises to do certain acts or refrain from doing certain acts
- "During the Term, Licensor shall make available 3 software engineers for a total of 15 engineer-days."

Implied Warranty of Merchantability

- Article sold is fit for the ordinary purposes for which such goods are to be used and conform to promises on package/label
- UCC 2-314: goods sold conform to ordinary standard of care and are of average grade, quality and value of similar goods sold under similar circumstances

Implied Warranty: Fitness for a Particular Purpose

- UCC 2-315: where seller at time of contracting has reason to know any particular purpose for which the goods are required, & buyer is relying on seller to furnish suitable goods, there is, unless excluded or modified, implied warranty that the goods shall be fit for such purpose

Warranties of Title & Non-infringement

- UCC 2-312(1) provides that in contract of sale, seller warrants that title shall be good and its transfer rightful, & goods shall be delivered free of undisclosed security interest
- 2-312(3) provides that if seller is "merchant" who regularly deals in goods of this kind, seller warrants that goods shall be free of any rightful infringement claim by a third party

Breach of Contract I

- Contractual promisor has option of performing or compensating other party for damages arising from nonperformance
- Usual remedy for breach of contract is money damages, unless promised matter is unique [*deliver a nuclear bomb*], in which case specific performance may be ordered (but it's rare)
- If breach is very substantial, possibility of rescission of contract & restitution (give benefit received by the *breaching* party)

Breach of Contract II

- Breach of covenant: as a promise, generally same as breach of contract: contract damages
- Warranty also a promise, breach ordinarily gives rise to action for contractual damages, amount sufficient to place non-breaching party in position he would have been in if facts were as warranted
- Generally, rescission of executory contracts permitted for breach of warranty

Indirect & Incidental Damages

- Indirect: damages that do not follow immediately from the act done, nor arise naturally or ordinarily from breach
- Incidental: (UCC 2-710) commercially reasonable charges or commissions incurred in stopping delivery or care & custody of goods after buyer's breach, re: return or resale of goods or otherwise from breach

Consequential Damages

- Damage, loss or injury not flowing directly or immediately from breach, but only from some results or consequences of act/breach
- Damages which arise from intervention of special circumstances, not ordinarily predictable
- Include any loss which seller had reason to know, cannot be adequately compensated by cover, and injury to person or property proximately resulting from breach of warranty (UCC 2-715(2))
- *Hadley v. Baxendale* (England, 1854)

Special Damages

- Damages which are the actual, but not necessary, result of breach/special condition
- Damages not contemplated by the parties when contract made, but which flow directly and immediately from breach and are reasonably foreseeable
- Must be specially pleaded & proved (FRCP 9(g))

Punitive or Exemplary Damages

- Damages on an increased scale, awarded to plaintiff above what will compensate him for property loss, where wrong/breach was aggravated by circumstances of malice, fraud, or willful misconduct
- Damages intended to compensate plaintiff for mental anguish or punish defendant for outrageous conduct; policy aim: punishment

Indemnification

- Undertaking where one agrees to compensate another upon occurrence of an anticipated loss, to make whole from loss already sustained
- Loss is shifted from actor who is only technically at fault to another who is primarily responsible
- Intended to avoid lawsuit to prove damages

IP Indemnification

- Recommended: Licensor will defend or settle any third-party claim against Customer that Software infringes a US copyright, trademark patent, trade secret (subject to exceptions)
- If the Territory expands beyond the United States, there will be pressure to cover any IP rights that originate in the Territory.
- *UETA:Uniform Electronic Transactions Act*
- UETA was approved for enactment by NCCUSL in 1999; enacted by 47 states inc. California (Cal. version has exceptions)

- Applies to electronic records & electronic signatures: record generated, communicated or stored by electronic means
- Applies to transactions between parties who agree to conduct same by electronic means

UCITA: Uniform Computer Information Transactions Act I

- UCITA was approved and recommended for enactment by NCCUSL in 1999
- UCITA would replace proposed UCC 2B, and would govern software licenses and transactions in computer information
- It has faced heavy opposition for a variety of reasons, and has been enacted only in MD & VA
- Would be good for software vendors

UCITA II

- Applies to "computer information": info. in electronic form obtained via use of computer or can be processed by a computer...including a copy of the info. & any documentation or packaging with copy
- Does not apply to sale of computer itself, excludes financial service transactions, sound recordings/broadcasts, motion pictures, most employment contracts, although has opt-in feature (and parties subject can opt-out)
- Resolves certain issues such as assent in online transactions that were awkward under UCC; "authenticated record" in place of "signed writing"

Signatures in the Electronic Age

- Statute of Frauds under UCC: signed writing required on contracts for sale of goods of/over $500; under UCITA, "authenticated record" if payment of/over $5000
- UCITA: authentication by means of electronic agent is valid; binds principal
- Courts generally accept click-wrap, shrink-wrap licenses as satisfying writing requirement of Statute of Frauds

Shrink-wrap & Click-wrap Licenses

- Shrink-wrap licenses: assent by opening &/or using program and not returning it
- Click-wrap: assent by clicking on "I agree" button
- Few cases on whether enforceable under writing/record and signature/authentication requirements, but assumed by most courts to satisfy Statute of Frauds
- Most courts assume they are valid agreements
- Under UCITA, they are "mass-market licenses": with end user, standard retail pricing, of type that usually appeals to general public

www.Aspatore.com

Aspatore Books is the largest and most exclusive publisher of C-Level executives (CEO, CFO, CTO, CMO, Partner) from the world's most respected companies and law firms. Aspatore annually publishes a select group of C-Level executives from the Global 1,000, top 250 law firms (Partners & Chairs), and other leading companies of all sizes. C-Level Business Intelligence™, as conceptualized and developed by Aspatore Books, provides professionals of all levels with proven business intelligence from industry insiders – direct and unfiltered insight from those who know it best – as opposed to third-party accounts offered by unknown authors and analysts. Aspatore Books is committed to publishing an innovative line of business and legal books, those which lay forth principles and offer insights that when employed, can have a direct financial impact on the reader's business objectives, whatever they may be. In essence, Aspatore publishes critical tools – need-to-read as opposed to nice-to-read books – for all business professionals.

Inside the Minds

The critically acclaimed *Inside the Minds* series provides readers of all levels with proven business intelligence from C-Level executives (CEO, CFO, CTO, CMO, Partner) from the world's most respected companies. Each chapter is comparable to a white paper or essay and is a future-oriented look at where an industry/profession/topic is heading and the most important issues for future success. Each author has been carefully chosen through an exhaustive selection process by the *Inside the Minds* editorial board to write a chapter for this book. *Inside the Minds* was conceived in order to give readers actual insights into the leading minds of business executives worldwide. Because so few books or other publications are actually written by executives in industry, *Inside the Minds* presents an unprecedented look at various industries and professions never before available.